MISSION IN THE U.S.A. SERIES

BIBLE & MISSION

Biblical Foundations and Working Models for Congregational Ministry

Editor
Wayne Stumme

AUGSBURG Publishing House • Minneapolis

BIBLE AND MISSION
Biblical Foundations and Working Models for Congregational Ministry

Library of Congress Cataloging-in-Publication Data

BIBLE AND MISSION.

(Mission in the U.S.A. series)
Bibliography: p.
1. Mission of the church. 2. Pastoral theology—
Lutheran Church. 3. Lutheran Church—Doctrines.
I. Stumme, Wayne, 1929- . II. Series.
BV601.8.B53 1986 86-22167
ISBN 0-8066-2237-7

Manufactured in the U.S.A. APH 10-0705

1 2 3 4 5 6 7 8 9 0 1 2 3 4 5 6 7 8 9

CONTENTS

CONTRIBUTORS

Paul Collinson-Streng, Pastor
Hidalgo Colonia Ministry
Edinburg, Texas

Terence E. Fretheim, Professor of Old Testament
and Dean of Academic Affairs
Luther Northwestern Theological Seminary
St. Paul, Minnesota

Debra Grant, Pastor
Pioneer Lutheran Church
Goodlettsville, Tennessee

Roy A. Harrisville, Professor of New Testament
Luther Northwestern Theological Seminary
St. Paul, Minnesota

Larry A. Hoffsis, Pastor
Epiphany Lutheran Church
Centerville, Ohio

Merlin H. Hoops, Professor of New Testament
Trinity Lutheran Seminary
Columbus, Ohio

Gordon S. Huffman Jr., John H. F. Kuder Professor of
Christian Mission
Trinity Lutheran Seminary
Columbus, Ohio

Donald H. Juel, Associate Professor of New Testament
Luther Northwestern Theological Seminary
St. Paul, Minnesota

BARBARA JURGENSEN, Assistant Professor of Old Testament and Contextual Education
Trinity Lutheran Seminary
Columbus, Ohio

LOWELL O. LARSON, Pastor
Vinje Lutheran Church
Willmar, Minnesota

LUIS ALBERTO PEREYRA, Pastor
Trinity Lutheran Church
Brooklyn, New York

WALTER E. PILGRIM, Professor of Religion and Director of the Lutheran Institute for Theological Education
Pacific Lutheran University
Tacoma, Washington

JOHN F. STEINBRUCK, Pastor
Luther Place Memorial Church
Washington, D.C.

WAYNE C. STUMME, Director
Institute for Mission in the U.S.A.
Trinity Lutheran Seminary
Columbus, Ohio

ISMAEL DE LA TEJERA, Pastor
Mision Luterana San Pablo
Weslaco, Texas

VIRGIL THOMPSON, Pastor
Our Savior Lutheran Church
Pinehurst, Idaho

EDITOR'S FOREWORD

Bible and Mission is the first volume in the series *Mission in the U.S.A.* Subsequent volumes will deal with other issues and challenges facing the church as it engages in mission in this nation.

Bible and Mission was prepared under the direction of the Institute for Mission in the U.S.A., a Lutheran project serving the mission of the church through research, education and training, and consultation. Offices of the institute are located at Trinity Lutheran Seminary, Columbus, Ohio.

INTRODUCTION

Wayne C. Stumme

> The Bible seeks people who can and will ask about God. It seeks those who are capable of letting their *little* questions—and which of them is *not* little in comparison?—merge in the *great* question about the cross, that is, about God.
>
> —*Karl Barth*[1]

The Time and Place for Mission

What has always been true has now become clearly evident to many American Christians. Whatever else may be said about the church, it is a company of persons sent by their Lord to others. That "sending" includes, but is not exhausted by, the dispatching of "missionaries" to distant parts of the world. Today the term *mission* has come to embrace the tasks of witness and service and advocacy which must be carried on in this land. The far-reaching changes of the last 40 years have altered dramatically our understanding of mission and, not least of all, our consciousness of what the church is commissioned to be and do in the United States of America.

Change never comes easily. The pain of going through one social upheaval after another, however, should not be allowed to obscure the positive outcomes of what has been happening to all of us. For example, persons once remote and strange have become people we know and love. Human needs we once ignored now stir us to practical deeds of compassion. Challenges both new and old are taken up in ways which would have surprised—and perhaps dismayed—members of an earlier generation. In brief, we have come to a lively appreciation of what it is to witness and serve as Christians in this society.

All of this is evidence of the rising missionary consciousness of the contemporary church. But what has the Bible to do with what has been described? The great Swiss theologian Karl Barth reminds us that the Bible is not only a book *about* mission but in a special way itself *is* mission. "The Bible seeks people who can and will ask about God." If that is true, how does the Bible continue to serve as witness and authority, correction and guide, for this generation of men and women sent by Christ to their contemporaries? That is the central concern which those who have contributed to this book intend to address.

This volume brings together reflections on our topic by men and women whose ministries are carried out in parish and seminary settings. None would claim completeness for what she or he has written; all understand that they speak as part of a community of faith in which honest dialog—that is, criticism as well as encouragement—must be fostered for the sake of faithful mission. Together they are offering to the church the results of their study and practical experience, those insights emerging from reverent scrutiny of the biblical texts and from thoughtful consideration of Christian discipleship in a variety of congregational settings. Their efforts, as will become apparent, are undergirded by loyalty to the church and shared faith in the Lord of the church. Common to all of them is genuine commitment to the mission of the church, at this time and in this place.

A Necessary Connection?

Do Bible and mission really belong together? It is important to probe this question more deeply. No one would deny the Bible's role in what may be called the "internal" life of the church. Preaching, the nurture of children, the education of members, the encouragement of piety—all of these activities are related to the Bible. Yet mission, it may be claimed, represents the "external" life of the church. How can the Bible help us commend the faith to those many others for whom its language is strange and its concepts remote from what they know? And how can this ancient collection of sacred writings prepare us for engagement with the questions and tragedies which a technologically advanced and conflict-ridden society throws at us day after day? The distance between the world of the Bible and our own seems so vast. Is the connection that we attempt to make between Bible and modern mission artificial and, quite simply, ineffective?

The question has been asked before, and by sincere and well-meaning Christians. Like us, they were concerned to commend the faith to those who did not believe. They, too, were aware of the difficulties in communicating the biblical message to those who were uninformed, indifferent, or hostile. So they asked themselves whether the leading philosophies, the accepted worldviews of their time, would offer a more promising point of contact. Was it not necessary to meet people "where they were" instead of trying to introduce them to the biblical understanding of their plight and prospects? Could not the disturbing voice of the Bible be muted, they wondered, or at least "translated" into a more congenial form of address? Or could not the encounter with the biblical message at least be postponed until folk were attracted by these other approaches and "eased" into the church? Such questions, and their implied answers, are not part of the distant past. They are heard—and with some insistence—from every part of the theological spectrum today.

Let us note that there is an opposing view. It was advanced by the pastor-theologian Karl Barth during a time of severe crisis for both society and church. For him the indispensable connection between Bible and mission was clear; the gospel witnessed to in the Bible opened the only way to authentic human freedom.

> In this world men and women find themselves to be imprisoned. In fact the more profoundly we become aware of the limited character of the possibilities which are open to us here and now, the more clear it is that we are farther from God, that our desertion of Him is more complete. . ., and the consequences of that desertion more vast than we had ever dreamed. [The union of men and women] with God is shattered so completely that they cannot even conceive of its restoration. Their sin is their guilt; their death is their destiny; their world is formless and tumultuous chaos, a chaos of the forces of nature and of the human soul; their life is illusion. This is the situation in which we find ourselves. The question "Is there then a God?" is therefore entirely relevant and indeed inevitable![2]

Other questions follow at once. What can break the chains of this universal slavery? Where is there hope for life in a world given over to death? Barth thundered in response:

> Now, it is the Gospel that opens up the possibility of this final perception, and, if this possibility is to be realized, all penultimate perceptions must be withdrawn from circulation. The Gospel speaks of God as He is. . . . It is pregnant with our complete conversion; for it announces the transformation of our creatureliness into freedom. It proclaims the forgiveness of our sins, the victory of life over death, in fact, the restoration of everything that has been lost. It is the signal, the fire-alarm, of a coming, new world.[3]

Bible and mission belong together, therefore, because mission always is concerned to communicate the knowledge of "God as he is," the God who liberates and forgives and restores a humanity unable to accomplish these things for itself. The biblical gospel, in other words, must animate our speaking and acting if they are to serve mission. And that gospel is the "signal," the "fire-alarm" of a new world coming, a world promised in the dying and rising of Jesus Christ. Mission is in the service of hope.

It is not that all of this can be communicated to our contemporaries without much effort and struggle. There is much we need to learn; we have a great deal of listening to do. We have to discover anew what awakens understanding and moves the will and touches feeling; we cannot turn back from what we find and retreat into comfortable enclaves of traditional religiosity. Our involvement in mission will not permit us to repeat familiar words in a manner which comforts us but confuses those not privy to their meaning. Our linking of Bible and mission, in other words, is not a disguised retreat to an earlier and narrower world of ethnically bounded religious culture. And why not? Because, as Barth reminds us, the gospel signals "a coming new world," a world which already challenges the way we view what is and what was. That new world is God's future, a future intended for a truly liberated humanity, a future the Bible calls the kingdom of God. The gospel sounds the trumpet announcing its coming; the gospel summons us to anticipate now the final and blessed transformation of all existence. "But God has promised new heavens and a new earth, where righteousness will be at home, and we wait for these!"[4] So declares the apostolic writer; so we believe, so we live.

How then does the Bible inform our understanding and practice of mission today? That question was put to the pastors and teachers who wrote this book. Their abundant gifts are apparent in these pages; the uniqueness of those different contexts in which they work and think has something to do with what they have discovered and wish to share. Each, in his or her own fashion, is aware of the human situation to which all speak and in which all live. Together, however, they declare that freedom, pardon, and restoration which mark God's victory in Christ, the victory of life over death. In this they are one in their commitment to the mission of the church.

The Beginning of a Mission Dialog

This book represents the speaking of men and women who first listened. They have heard the words of Scripture; they have attended to the voices that spoke in congregations and the larger society. Their own speaking is directed to all who have taken up tasks of mission in this land. For their part, the authors welcome response from those who read these pages. Such a dialog can only strengthen the mission of the church.

How can we best describe the church in mission? Perhaps less in static and more in dynamic terms; perhaps not so much as an institution but more as a movement; perhaps the church in mission is less like a rock and more like a river. Such language may help us appropriate what the writers of this book have to give us. They offer their insights, interpretations, experiences, reflections, and suggestions. They do not provide final answers, but want to enter into conversation with others who take seriously the church's missionary vocation.

Consider the chapters dealing with the theme of mission in the Bible. Ancient Israel had its own theology of mission, mission which was directed beyond God's covenant nation to all peoples. This is part of the rich heritage which the church has received from the Old Testament. The evangelist Luke continues the story of God's saving purpose in history. That history comes to its climax in the Christ, whose own ministry brought hope to the poor and the outcasts. As a consequence of his death and resurrection, the apostolic community took up its mission to all of humanity.

The apostle Paul interpreted the event of Jesus Christ as the mission of God to win back God's alienated creation. The mission of the church, therefore, cannot simply be identified with the mission of God, but it participates in the divine purpose as it proclaims the saving righteousness of God in Christ. John's Gospel offers an "indirect" but powerful mission theology. The "sentness" of the church and the Christological focus of all that it does are dominant notes in the Johannine presentation.

The concreteness of the mission calling of the church is stressed by the evangelist Matthew. Christians are to share God's own concern for the entire world but at the same time not to neglect the responsibilities which are theirs as members of specific communities of faith. Discipleship is not only winning others through the proclamation of the gospel but caring for those in desperate need.

These and other biblical emphases are taken up in chapter 6, which summarizes the impact of the Bible on modern theologies of mission. Many of these theologies originated in churches of the Third World, and their appropriation of the Bible has stressed long-neglected themes, such as the poor, deliverance for the oppressed, the threat of idolatry, and hope in history. The unifying motif of the kingdom of God brings together these major emphases of contemporary mission theology.

The remarkably diverse experiences of congregations in a variety of contexts provide a kind of "commentary" on the biblical presentations. An inner-city congregation discovered the relevance of the Bible through approaches which reached persons in all age groups and cultural backgrounds. A large congregation in a midwestern town found its nurture and outreach and service inspired by the Bible. Believing that mission was carried out primarily through what its members did in their everyday "callings," this church placed a good deal of emphasis on biblical instruction.

Working among the poorest of the poor in the American Southwest, a Hispanic congregation had to deal with widespread biblical illiteracy within a largely unevangelized population. From their experience came a strong emphasis upon the Bible and the Holy Spirit and upon the renewal of life on the part of the converted. A rural congregation in the western part of the nation saw itself facing the crises of authority, identity, and community. By restoring to its members "an intelligent and affectionate use of the Bible" it also prepared them for their participation in the mission of the church.

What meaning can the Bible have in a multicultural congregation in a major eastern metropolis? The answer: the Bible provided fundamental theological resources for dealing with the issues of racism, class discrimination, and homelessness. Through a vision inspired by the Bible, "Christ is seen alive, walking daily in the streets as God's own expression of love, hope, and salvation." A young pastor introduces a mission congregation in a southern state, and recounts the problems and possibilities which arise when the Bible was used in such a setting. Questions of interpretation had a direct impact upon mission outreach and the proclamation of the gospel.

A center-city congregation in our nation's capital rediscovered the meaning of biblical hospitality. It reaches out to the homeless and destitute and offers them "a place where our own itinerant Savior can be at home and welcome outcasts." It is from the Bible that a suburban congregation received its impetus to mission. Here, too, the practice of hospitality and the willingness to "bear one another's burdens" grew out of a new missionary consciousness.

The experience, study, and reflection contained in these chapters are intended to encourage those many men and women who are engaged in the work of mission in this nation. At the same time, this book is meant to serve as prod and stimulus to others, whose sense of the church's missionary vocation needs to be awakened. Adult groups in local congregations may want to study the biblical chapters as preparation for the framing of a mission statement. Existing mission policies and practices may be measured against the concerns of the biblical writers. The chapter on biblical motifs in contemporary mission theology can introduce congregations to the startling biblical insights of Third World Christians.

Part II of this volume, which recounts the impact of the Bible upon mission in a variety of congregations, can be especially helpful. The experiences recounted by the pastors of these faith communities are not meant to be understood as models of mission which can simply be applied in other contexts. Nevertheless, their discoveries may point out to others dimensions of mission which they have previously overlooked. The authors' attempts to ground what they are doing in the biblical Word should be a reminder to all that Christian practice should unambiguously reflect Christian conviction. And, not least in importance, their efforts to open up new areas on the frontiers of mission deserve our attention and emulation.

We commend this book to all who serve the mission of the church in our American society. The pages which follow will speak at some length about understanding and doing that mission. Essential as that is, there is an awareness which precedes all of our thought and activity. Mission has to do with our human asking about God, that is, our asking about the deepest meaning of our own existence in the light of the purposes of God. And the question about God, we have been reminded, is the great question about the cross. The reality and the power of all Christian mission, therefore, is Jesus Christ, crucified and risen, Lord and Savior. He, sent by the Father to us, sends us to others.

PART I

BIBLICAL PERSPECTIVES ON MISSION

1

THE UNDERSTANDING OF MISSION IN THE OLD TESTAMENT[1]

Terence E. Fretheim

> Sing to the Lord, bless his name;
>   tell of his salvation from day to day.
> Declare his glory among the nations,
>   his marvelous works among all the peoples. . . .
> Say among the nations, "The Lord reigns!"
>
> (Ps. 96:2-3, 10)

It is difficult to imagine a clearer call to mission than this! It should be crystal clear: long before Jesus was born, God was concerned about mission. Round the entire world, since time began, God has been present and at work among all peoples, moving them in every conceivable way towards God's redemptive goals.

God chose Israel to begin that work in an articulate way, as Psalm 96 and other passages soon to be discussed make clear. Israel's election was never for the sake of the people of Israel alone. In the words of Ps. 67:1-2, God blessed Israel so that God's "way may be known upon earth, God's saving power among all nations."

It is thus clear that the idea and the practice of mission are not born with Jesus or the church, though this is a common perception (in fact, the notion of mission is not even peculiar to the Judeo-Christian tradition, cf. Buddhism). The task of mission and a theology of mission were inherited from the people of Israel. What happened in Jesus was that this task was raised to a new level of articulateness and intensity and eschatological urgency.

The New Testament states explicitly that the mission to the nations was a fulfillment of the Old Testament Scriptures (Luke 24:47; Rom. 15:8-12; Gal. 3:8; Acts 13:47; 15:14-18). The early church thus considered mission to be a part of the purposes of God from the beginning, and saw this as a point of continuity with the faith of the Old Testament people. The church inherited the mission articulated in the Old Testament.

The church needs to be alert to the fact that, even with all its efforts, God still works in more independent ways on God's mission. For example, on a visit to Japan, a country the population of which is less than 1% Christian, I was surprised at how God's word was being articulated in not very churchly ways. Thus, on a Sunday afternoon in December, in the big department stores on the Ginza in Tokyo, I heard the message of Christmas coming through in very public and remarkably clear ways. Not in the words of some Christian preaching on the street corner or handing out Bibles or tracts, but in the commercialization of Christmas, in a form much more prominent than in our increasingly crecheless land. The carols of Christmas, in both English and Japanese, were ringing out through the ever-present Musak system. And I marveled as I heard words such a these go bouncing around the eardrums of the largely non-Christian crowds pressing through the shops: "Christ, the Savior, is born; Christ, the Savior, is born!"

The Old Testament witness to mission continues to speak this word to us: in ways not explicitly Christian, and certainly not very churchly, God is about the business of mission in our world, as God was in Israel's world. God uses ways and means that we might view as improbable or even inappropriate, and certainly often quite "secular," to get that word through. As in the pre-Christian world, so also in the "Christian" world God is at work on God's saving will for the world.

We now need to explore some of the more particular ways in which these concerns are expressed in Old Testament materials. We pay special attention to the Psalms, not least because they are not given as much attention as other texts (e.g., Isaiah 40–66) in studies of Israel's understanding of mission. We first speak of aspects of Israel's theology of mission, and then conclude with a brief picture of Israel's practice of mission. Mission is understood throughout as *speaking or embodying the Word of God to others, either within Israel or beyond its national boundaries*.

God's Suffering Presence

The source and the heartbeat of the understanding of mission in the Old Testament is its understanding of God. The God of Israel is the God of the entire world. We take a look at two perspectives on this God: suffering presence and loving lordship.

"Do not I fill heaven and earth? says the Lord" (Jer. 23:24; cf. Amos 9:2-6; Ps. 139:7-15). Where there is world, there is God; where there is God, there is world. God's presence interpenetrates all aspects of the life of the world. Where God is present, God is active, working toward those purposes of salvation for the whole world. Thus, all people in the world have experienced God, in election (cf. Isa. 45:1,4), judgment (cf. Amos 1–2), and blessing:

> Are you not like the Ethiopians to me,
>   O people of Israel? says the Lord.
> Did I not bring up Israel from the land of Egypt,
>   and the Philistines from Caphtor
>   and the Syrians from Kir?
>
> (Amos 9:7)

The Philistines and Syrians (as well as others) may not have realized it, of course, but God's activity has had an effect on their lives. This ought to have a dramatic effect on how we think about mission: we need to find ways to touch base with the experience of God which people have—in fact, had—before we showed up with the Bible in our hands. Thus, for example, what experiences of the transcendent might one be able to point to in the lives of people, such as an experience of self-giving love, totally undeserved?

In the Old Testament, God is revealed as one who not only enters into the suffering life of Israel (e.g., Exod. 2:23-25; 3:7), but also into the suffering life of all. For example, God enters into the mournful situation of non-Israelite peoples (e.g., Isa. 15:5; 16:9,11; Jer. 48:30-36):

I know his insolence, says the Lord. . . .
Therefore I wail for Moab;
  I cry out for all Moab;
  for the men of Kir-heres I mourn.
More than for Jazer I weep for you.

(Jer. 48:30-32)

This demonstrates Israel's recognition of the breadth of God's care and concern for the suffering of the world, whoever they might be. Israel has no monopoly on God's empathy. We see in such texts the scope, consistency, and the commonality of God's suffering presence with all.

The Old Testament witnesses to a God who truly shares in the life of the world. God has chosen not to remain serenely above all that makes for life; God has entered into worldly reality and made it God's own. Contrary to some Advent and Christmas sermons, the Incarnation is not the point at which God entered into the life of the world. The Old Testament witnesses to that activity of God as well. The Christ event witnesses to God's becoming flesh in a full human life, and that is a culmination of God's ways revealed to Israel.

God's Loving Lordship

God is the king of all the earth. . . .
  God reigns over the nations. . . .
The princes of the peoples gather
  as the people of the God of Abraham.

(Ps. 47:7-9)

If God is Lord of all—and God is—then God's love and saving purposes are for all. For the Old Testament people, God's kingdom is not confined to the land of Palestine. God's reign extends over all. And it is precisely because God is Lord of all that the people of God are called to bring the word of that God to all peoples (Ps. 96:2-3).

From the rising of the sun to its setting
  the name of the Lord is to be praised.

(Ps. 113:3; cf. Mal. 1:11)

The praise of the Lord knows no boundaries. When at times Israel sought to identify God's kingdom with the Israelite kingdom, it failed to recognize this world-wide scope of God's Lordship.

Because of all that God has accomplished on behalf of all the peoples of the earth, Israel calls upon them to "come and see what God has done" (Ps. 66:4), and to sing praises to God (e.g., Ps. 117:1; 66:1; 68:32; 96:7-9; 99:1-2):

> Let the nations be glad and sing for joy,
> for thou dost judge the peoples with equity
> and guide the nations upon earth.
>
> (Ps. 67:4)

The judging and guiding hand of God moves among all the peoples, and because of that they are called to sing songs of gladness. Israel recognizes that it is not the only people on earth which owes praise to God for all that God has done. Hence, the call goes out from Israel for everyone to praise God for such bountiful blessings.

Even more, the Old Testament affirms strongly that God, in relating to the world, is *lovingly* committed to it. While the manifestations of God's love in Israel are manifold and clear, they are also evident outside of Israel. For example, in Psalm 136 we see God's love being celebrated for its evidence in God's actions throughout the world. God's love is seen to be the driving force behind all of God's works, in nature as well as history. In other psalms, we hear of the entire earth being filled with the steadfast love of God (Ps. 33:5; 36:5; 85:10-12; 119:64):

> Thy steadfast love is great to the heavens,
> thy faithfulness to the clouds.
>
> (Ps. 57:10; cf. 108:4)

Because of this, the people of God promise to "give thanks. . . among the peoples" and "sing praises. . .among the nations" (Ps. 57:9; cf. 108:3). The people of God see how God's world-wide love is showered on all, how God's faithfulness is evident in all the world; hence they cannot but make articulate to others the source of that love. Israel is to proclaim God's praises precisely because God's love fills the earth, and is not confined to Israel.

Covenant language also finds such world-wide connections in a number of passages. For example, in Genesis 9 the covenant which God establishes after the flood is a covenant with every creature (vv. 9-10). This, of course, is a pre-Israelite promise, so that God makes a commitment to all, human and nonhuman. God is concerned about bringing humanity—indeed the world—from chaos to order, from fragmentation to family. God's work among all is based on an irrevocable commitment and is moved and motivated by God's love for everyone.

Because Israel has been the recipient of this love in very specific ways, and knows the God from whom this love has come, it is called upon to show forth that love in its everyday life.

Gratitude and Mission

> Come and hear. . .,
> and I will tell you what [God] has done for me.
>
> (Ps. 66:16)

One of the important types of psalms is the song of thanksgiving, wherein the worshiper gives thanks to God for some deliverance which has been experienced. This song is closely related to another type of psalm, often called the lament. Commonly, at the end of these laments, there is a vow of praise:

> I will tell of thy name to my brethren;
> in the midst of the congregation I will praise thee.
>
> (Ps. 22:22)

In this vow the worshipers promise to give praise to God, to make God's name great. The most appropriate context in which this can happen is among a group of people. Most simply, this is a vow to tell other people all that God has done on their behalf. Gratitude to God is thus expressed not simply *to God,* as important as that is; it is to be expressed *in the presence of others*. Gratitude is giving testimony to others regarding what God has done.

> I have told the glad news of deliverance
> in the great congregation;
> lo, I have not restrained my lips. . . .

> I have not hid thy saving help within my heart,
> I have spoken of thy faithfulness and thy salvation.
>
> (Ps. 40:9-10)

While this witness is commonly given in the midst of a congregation of believers (Ps. 22:22; 109:30), the vow is also stated in terms that have the whole world in view:

> I will give thanks to thee, O Lord, among the peoples;
> I will sing praises to thee among the nations.
>
> (Ps. 57:9; cf. 145:11-12)

> For this [deliverance] I will extol thee, O Lord, among the nations,
> and sing praises to thy name.
>
> (Ps. 18:49)

Psalm 22:27 (cf. 86:9; 102:15) envisions that such testimony will have worldwide effects, as

> All the ends of the earth shall remember
> and turn to the Lord;
> and all the families of the nations
> shall worship before him.

Moreover, while a specific worship service when such testimony would be given is often in view, gratitude is intended to be characteristic of one's entire life:

> Then my tongue shall tell of thy righteousness
> and of thy praise all the day long.
>
> (Ps. 35:28; cf. 71:22-24)

The witness to what God has done is not simply to be reported once, but "day after day" (Ps. 61:8). It must be continually expressed in the entirety of one's life.

It is such an everyday stance of gratitude that is to inform not only one's verbal witness, but also one's acting witness. It is in the book of Deuteronomy in particular where this is stressed:

> [The Lord] executes justice for the fatherless and the widow, and loves the sojourner, giving him food and clothing. Love the sojourner therefore; for you were sojourners in the land of Egypt.
>
> (Deut. 10:18-19; cf. Exod. 22:21; 23:9)

Because of all that God has done on behalf of the people of Israel, they are to shape their life in such a way as to imitate those actions of God on behalf of the poor and oppressed (see Lev. 19:10; 23:22; Deut. 14:29; 24:19). Witness, therefore, does not simply take the form of words, as important as that is; it also takes the form of concrete action. The shape of one's life gives testimony to the God who has dealt so bountifully with God's people. Evangelism and social action are not separable forms of witness; they are two sides of the same coin. Mission takes the form of both words and actions (Rom. 15:18).

Election, Servanthood, and Mission

The Bible opens, not with the story of Israel, but with the story of the world and all of its peoples. Israel first makes its appearance in the Table of Nations in Genesis 10. Here Israel is placed in the midst of secular history; Israel has the same status as all the other peoples. When Israel is chosen in Abraham, that election has meaning only in terms of these "families of the earth" (Gen. 12:3) out of which it has been chosen. Israel is elected by God for the sake of all these other families, that God's blessing might come to all of them through what Israel is and does. For Israel, election was for mission: "by you all the families of the earth shall be blessed." Even in those actions, where God may be said to be most concerned about establishing the people of Israel, it is "so that my name may be declared throughout all the earth" (Exod. 9:16).

Jump the centuries to Jeremiah and one finds a comparable focus for the election of the prophet:

> Before you were born I consecrated you;
> I appointed you a prophet to the nations.
>
> (Jer. 1:5)

Jeremiah is chosen by God, not simply as a prophet to Israel, but as a prophet "to the nations." There is thus a scope to God's acts of choosing which embraces the world in terms of its purpose. God wants the world for God's people. Prophets like Jeremiah witness to a boundary-breaking God, showing that God's concern is for every creature, not just Israel. The prophets speak out against all uncritical understandings of election, all unfaithfulness that insists upon centering on oneself in relationship with God, every absorbing concern for one's own identity as the elect.

Move into the next century, and we see the prophet of the exile speak once again of the electing work of God in these terms.

> Behold my servant, whom I uphold,
> my chosen, in whom my soul delights;
> I have put my Spirit upon him,
> he will bring forth justice to the nations. . . .
> I have given you as a [mediator of my] covenant to the people,
> a light to the nations.
>
> (Isa. 42:1,6; cf. 49:6)

However one identifies the servant, whether as Israel or a prophetic figure, the horizon of God's election is the nations of the world. At the same time, the concern for these nations was not narrowly focused on conversion, at least as that is usually conceived. The servant is to bring forth justice, "to open the eyes that are blind, to bring out the prisoners from the dungeon" (Isa. 42:7). It is service on behalf of every aspect of the lives of the peoples of the world. It is this comprehensive understanding of salvation which, through the servant, is to "reach to the end of the earth" (49:6). Salvation is not confined to religious areas of life; it includes matters of hunger, and peace, and justice.

Mission is not confined to saving souls or making converts (in fact, it is striking how that kind of language seems too narrow for Israel's understanding of mission). Rather, mission must embody a concern for the whole person, spiritual and physical. Even more, mission is in the interests of total redemption: body, mind, spirit, earth, world, universe (Rom. 8:19). The boundary between sacred and secular is rent asunder in Israel's understanding of mission.

Being a "light to the nations" means to assume an exemplary role in the world (see Matt. 5:14-16). As the peoples of the world see what Israel has become, they too will sing praises to God. How the people of God "appear" to others makes a difference; they are attracted or repelled (or just plain indifferent) with respect to their God.

The meaning of mission in the Old Testament reaches its clearest expression in these suffering servant passages, and is reinforced by a variety of other texts in Isaiah (Isa. 44:5; 51:4-5). God formed this people "that they might declare my praise" (Isa. 43:21). But it is the servant who embodies the mission of God, and hence suffering is seen to be integral to mission. The purpose of Israel's election is servanthood, suffering service on behalf of all the nations of the world.

As Israel looked ahead, the future had an inclusive character. God's future included not just Israel but all peoples. Mission was not a salvage operation for a few select ones; it was a vision which encompassed the world (see Isa. 2:1-4; 19:16-25; 25:6-9; Jer. 3:17; 12:14-17; 16:19-21):

> To me every knee shall bow,
> every tongue shall swear.
> (Isa. 45:23; cf. Phil. 2:10-11)

> All the nations thou hast made shall come
> and bow down before thee, O Lord,
> and shall glorify thy name.
> (Ps. 86:9; cf. Zeph. 2:11)

The Practice of Mission

It is very important to remember in thinking about Israel's practice of mission that we not define this activity solely in terms of "foreign missions." Many of the above-noted texts give evidence for considerable mission activity on Israel's part among its own people, in both word and deed. Israel's lively theology of mission constantly propelled Israel to active witness among the very mixed religious population of which it was a part for so many centuries (see 2 Chron. 2:17).

With respect to the vehicles for mission, Israel was remarkably broad in its strategies. Basic was the proclamation of the Word of God, including the articulation of the gospel as well as the prophetic critique. Deeds of love and mercy were integral to any wholistic approach to mission. Dialog had a role to play, as did example. But, in everything, the word was servanthood, the giving of self on behalf of the salvific will of God for the world.

Regarding "world mission," it is difficult to determine the extent to which Israel actually engaged in the practice of mission outside of its own boundaries. As has been the case in the history of Christianity, there were no doubt times of greater and lesser activity, depending upon the nature of the internal situation. Certainly the theological perspectives are present in sufficient quantity and depth that one ought not be surprised at considerable mission activity outside the land of Palestine. The Old Testament sources by their very nature (e.g., Psalms), however, do not lend themselves to reporting about such matters. This has led to some differences among scholars in their assessment of Israel's practice of mission. It seems clear to this writer, however, that George Mendenhall's judgment is on target: "there is some reason to believe that the Old Testament faith was at the beginning an active missionary religion."[2] At times, Israel also assumed a more passive role.

Thus, for example, from earliest times foreigners had been incorporated into the community of faith (see Exod. 12:38). It is likely that many Canaanites converted to Yahwism during the Conquest (see, e.g., Josh. 2:11; 6:25; 9; 2 Sam. 6:10-11; 11:11; 15:19-22). Joshua 24 presents a religious occasion which urges outsiders to "choose this day whom you will serve" (v. 15). Ruth 1:16 speaks of foreigners coming to know the God of Israel, and sets that sort of understanding within the period of the Judges. The extent to which the conquests of David and the ventures of Solomon resulted in conversions to Yahwism is unknown, though Pss. 2:10-11; 87:4-6; and 1 Kings 8:41-43 beseech the Lord to hear the prayer of the foreigner (who has heard of the Lord in "a far country") who comes to pray in the temple, so that all the peoples of the earth may come to know the Lord. The activities of some early prophets among non-Israelites, particularly Elisha (see 2 Kings 5; 8:7-15; cf. 17:26-28; 1 Kings 17:12), move in similar directions.

While the prophetic oracles against the nations (e.g., Amos 1–2; Isaiah 13–23; Jeremiah 46–51; Ezekiel 25–32) are of uncertain meaning, there is no inherent reason why they could not refer to a mission activity among peoples such as we see in the book of Jonah. The book of Jonah must be based on known mission activity on Israel's part. But it is particularly in the literature that stems from the Babylonian exile that we hear of foreigners being incorporated into the Israelite community (e.g., Isa. 56:3-8). By the time of the postexilic Mal. 1:11, it could be said that "from the rising of the sun to its setting my name is great among the nations" (cf. Isa. 66:18-21). Finally, the missionary activity of Judaism in the intertestamental period is well known (cf. Matt. 23:15). It is likely that this activity is based on the theology of mission we have seen in the Old Testament, and patterned after known practices inherited from more ancient times.

In Israel, through these many pre-Christian centuries, there was an active missionary enterprise based upon a sophisticated theology of mission. The church should be more grateful for what it has inherited, and recognize that God continues to be about mission activity in ways not directly associated with the church.

2

LUKE: HISTORY AND MISSION

Walter E. Pilgrim

Introduction

The author of Luke-Acts is the historian of the early church; the second volume of his two-volume work provides us with the only church history in the New Testament. We also learn of Luke's historical interest from his two prefaces (Luke 1:1-4; Acts 1:1-2). Like contemporary authors of his day, both sacred and secular, Luke composes prefaces dedicated to a Greek patron (in Luke's case, Theophilus), in which he sets forth the objectives of both volumes. He claims to be in touch with reliable sources ("eyewitnesses and ministers of the word") and to have the ability to write an "orderly account" of the events connected with Jesus of Nazareth (Luke 1:2-3). His purpose is the confirmation of what Theophilus has heard, confirmation intended either to convert the patron or, more likely, to strengthen his faith. (Both interpretations are possible. We would like to have more information. Is it an evangelistic writing or an "in-house" Christian document? I favor the theory that Luke writes to a newly converted God-fearer or proselyte.)

In book one, we have the foundational history concentrating on the story of Jesus from his birth to his resurrection/ascension. In book two, we have the continuing history of this story as it is carried out in the life of the early church. The preface to Acts (1:1-2) links the two together: "In the first book, O Theophilus, I have dealt with all that

Jesus began to do and teach, until the day when he was taken up." What follows is the sequel to the original story, the Spirit-filled saga of the witnesses to Jesus who continue his presence and work in the world.

Luke records the initial history of Jesus and the church in a faithful and intelligible way. Of all the evangelists, he is the one most alert to secular history, and to the worldly powers that seem to control its destiny. Luke alone makes reference to a census at Jesus' birth (2:1-2), and dates the ministries of John the Baptist and Jesus in the tenure of Emperor Tiberius, Pontius Pilate, Herod Antipas, and Annas and Caiaphas (3:1-2). Throughout Acts he demonstrates wide and accurate knowledge of the provinces and cities with their various administrators in the far-flung Roman empire, stretching around the Mediterranean and beyond. Historians may debate some details, and Luke may tend to idealize past history, but his overall presentation appears to be that of a reliable historian of the first century (like the Greek historian Thucydides, or the Jewish historian Josephus).

However—and this is important for our purposes—Luke is above all a Christian historian. He writes history, but a special kind of history, "salvation history." This is history which sees God redemptively at work in human history. For Luke this "salvation-history" began with the history of Israel, came to its fulfillment in the time of Jesus, and continues in the history of the early apostles and the church until the return of Christ and the establishment of the new age. Because this is sacred history, Luke underscores the divine purpose which lies behind the story of Jesus and the early church. A key Greek word is *dei* (Luke 24:26,46), the divine "must" (RSV) that determines what takes place; or Luke can refer to the predetermined plan and purpose of God (Acts 2:23), or the fulfillment of Scripture (Luke 24:46; Acts 3:18), or the role of the Spirit that empowers the life of Jesus and the early church. This is history going some place, history under divine providence, history with purpose and meaning that transcends the capriciousness and ordinariness of secular history.

This is a magnificent story and challenge that Luke presents. He shows us God at work in human history, centering in the story of Jesus. This was God's rescue mission for the world. It transcends all other events of world history, and now, by recording it, he invites his readers—you and me—to share in the history and the mission. By responding, we become, as it were, coworkers with God in the shaping of God's redemptive purposes for the world. Let us see more clearly how Luke integrates his vision of history and mission in the dual story of Jesus and the church.

Foundational History: The Mission of Jesus in the Gospel of Luke

The main outline of the Lukan story of Jesus' mission is clearly discernible in Luke's Gospel: literary preface (1:1-4), birth narratives (1:5—2:52), ministry of John and Jesus in Galilee (3:1—19:27), and Jesus' suffering, death, and resurrection in Jerusalem (19:28—24:53). In the central section Luke also inserts a long travel narrative (9:51—18:31), which depicts Jesus on the way to Jerusalem. Much of this outline follows Mark's Gospel. Commentators agree, however, that one text is especially crucial for understanding Luke's presentation, Luke 4:14-30. In this text, as in no other, Luke sets forth the purpose and scope of Jesus' mission. Observe three things. (1) Jesus' historic mission is interpreted as the fulfillment of Isa. 61:1-2. He is the one anointed by the Spirit to proclaim good news to the poor, the captive, the blind, and the oppressed, and to announce the jubilee year of God's favor. This prophetic interpretation of Jesus' mission is then depicted and fulfilled in the remainder of the Gospel. (2) Jesus' experience of rejection by his own people foreshadows the ultimate rejection in his suffering and death. (3) Jesus recalls God's previous movement from Jews to Gentiles in the stories of Elijah and Elisha, which again foretell the story of the church of Acts. What we have in this text, therefore, is the whole outline of the Gospel and Acts as Luke unfolds it.

Jesus' Ministry of Good News to the Poor

The citation of Isaiah 61 sounds the theme of Jesus' earthly mission. At his baptism, he is anointed by the Spirit of God to carry out his ministry as the anointed Son/servant. A comparison of Luke's story of Jesus' baptism with those of Mark and Matthew quickly shows how Luke focuses especially on the Spirit's descent and infilling (3:21-22; 4:1, 14). In the Spirit's power, Jesus enacts his divinely given mandate to bring good news to the poor.

Already in the Lukan birth narratives this theme is sounded. These beautiful stories echo with the joy and wonder of inbreaking salvation. The three hymns of Mary, Zechariah, and Simeon, which have found their way into our liturgies, are bursting with the good news that God's promised redemption has arrived. God "has visited and redeemed his people. . .and has raised up a horn of salvation for us in the house of his servant David" (Luke 1:68, Zechariah). Or "mine eyes have seen thy salvation which thou has prepared in the presence of all peoples, a light for revelation to the Gentiles, and for glory to thy people Israel" (2:30-32, Simeon). But Mary's hymn expresses the singular meaning of Jesus' coming best of all, and most provocatively: God's "mercy is on those who fear him," and what this means is that God is at work creating a great reversal in human history. The wealthy and powerful are brought low and the poor and humble are raised up. "He has put down the mighty from their thrones, and exalted those of low degree; he has filled the hungry with good things, and the rich he has sent empty away" (1:52-53). This great reversal of God's redemption is then enacted in the birth of Jesus, where God enters human history in lowly form (Mary, shepherds, manger) and so incarnates oneself among the poor and lowly. A divine revolution in history is on the way.

This theme continues in the story of Jesus' public ministry in the Gospel. The good news to the poor now becomes manifest in Jesus' words and deeds. Commentators have repeatedly noted how Luke draws special attention to Jesus' redemptive encounters with the disadvantaged. This includes a wide circle of people. There are first of all the "outcasts and sinners." The picture of Jesus as "friend of tax collectors and sinners" comes chiefly from Luke's portrait (5:29-32; 7:34; 15:1-2). These sinners receive acceptance and God's unconditional forgiveness. The heart of the gospel for Luke is contained in chap. 15 and other parables of God's boundless mercy, which Jesus embodies in his ministry. Repentance and forgiveness open the way to God and make persons to be sons and daughters of the kingdom. There are also the sick, whose healing of body is a sign of the kingdom's presence. Since sickness and sin were inseparably related in the first century, the restoration to health conveys healing and forgiveness, though Jesus rejects the equation of illness with specific sins.

There are the poor and needy, too. Here a special word needs to be said about Luke's presentation of the poor. Our tendency in the past has been to understand the poor metaphorically or spiritually. There is some precedence for this in Matthew's Gospel (Matt. 5:6, "poor in spirit") and in Jewish religion (*anawim* = "pious poor"). Luke, too, is concerned with the inner spirit of humility before God and humanity (1:52). But Luke's understanding of the poor cannot simply be spiritualized. In fact, in the Sermon on the Plain (6:20-26) and the majority of places where the poor are mentioned, Luke has the genuinely poor and needy in mind. These are persons living in poverty, economically and socially oppressed, victims of injustice and deprivation. To these persons, suffering real hunger and thirst, and caught in the cycle of poverty, Jesus speaks a word of hope. The kingdom is theirs, and this means a new community of hope already here, and a promised reversal in the age to come. At the same time, Luke's Jesus issues words of warning to the rich and comfortable, and invites them to share their abundance with the poor. Both the Sermon with its beatitudes and woes, and numerous striking parables and stories make this point with telling clarity (16:19-31; 12:13-21; 14:7-14; 19:1-10).

And there are the women, persons on the margin of humanity in their time, treated by Jesus with refreshing and surprising dignity and worth. In the gospel story Luke delights in calling attention to their prominence. The birth narratives feature Mary and Elizabeth and Anna, and show Mary as the prime example of one who believes (1:38-45). During his ministry, Jesus rescues victims of male lust and power (7:36-50), teaches women the one thing needful (10:38-42), and has a following of women who support him (8:1-3). Women are the only witnesses to his crucifixion and the first witnesses to the empty tomb (23:49,55; 24:1-11), women are among the company of disciples in the Upper Room at Pentecost (Acts 1:12-14; 2:1), and the most surprising is Jesus' use of female imagery for God (Luke 15:8-10). Only among the circle of the Twelve are there no women. Jesus regards women as full partners in the human race and in the family of God. How different this was from his surroundings, and even from the church which followed him down through the centuries.

What this demonstrates is that the good news of the kingdom proclaimed by Jesus reaches out to persons without limit. All are included as objects of God's grace and compassion. Especially does this mean good news for the disadvantaged, those on the margins, sinners, the sick, the suffering, and the poor. Where need exists, Jesus reaches out as God's anointed servant/Son to forgive, to heal, and to make whole.

Jesus' Path through Suffering to Glory

Jesus' initial sermon at Nazareth (Luke 4:16-30) also gives us a clue to understanding Jesus' mission of suffering and death. His rejection by his own townspeople heralds the end of his life on a cross. This fate is only hinted at the beginning, but it soon becomes apparent that Jesus' claim to speak and act in God's name and with a uniquely given authority will meet with increasing resistance, rejection, and hostility. Like the prophets of old, his fate will inevitably lead to Jerusalem and death (13:34-35).

Luke created a special way to warn the reader of the final events in Jesus' rejection. We mentioned earlier the long travel narrative in the Gospel (9:51—18:31). Throughout this section, Jesus is on his way to Jerusalem, and he periodically announces his approaching suffering, death, and resurrection (9:51; 13:31; 17:25; 18:31-33). Luke 9:51 provides the interpretive key. Here we learn that Jesus sets his face to go to Jerusalem (a divine *must*) in order "to be received up." Behind this expression is the whole complex of Jesus' suffering, death, resurrection and exaltation. That is to say, Jesus' journey in life goes through suffering to glory. His destination is the coming kingdom, but the path can be gained only through suffering. No crown, we say, without the cross. That is the distinct way Luke describes the subsequent course of Jesus' life. It ends with his resurrection and ascension/exaltation to the Father as the Messiah and Lord (Acts 2:36). Yet, the reality of sin makes the cross the gateway to victory, and death the path to life. This point is taught plainly by the risen Lord himself at the conclusion of the Gospel: "Was it not necessary (*dei*) that the Christ should suffer these things and enter into his glory?" (24:26).

What is true for Jesus is also true for those who continue Jesus' mission. Their promise is the coming kingdom, the glory of sharing the inheritance of sons and daughters in the kingdom. Already now they share in the promise through forgiveness and love and joy and courage and all the gifts of the Spirit alive in the community of faith. But the full share is still future, still promise. In the present, there is the reality of sin and rejection and hostility, the result of a society and values that stand opposed to God's truth embodied in Christ. So the Christian way in the present is always inseparable from tension, conflict, potential suffering, and martyrdom.

This will become most apparent as Luke narrates the continuing story of the church in Acts. It is already visible in the Gospel. In the Lukan apocalypse (end-time teaching, chap. 21), he expands on the Markan version to describe the type of treatment Christ's disciples will receive after his death. In Luke 21:12-19, they are told to expect to be handed over to "synagogues and prisons" and to be "brought before kings and governors for my sake." This sounds like the stories in Acts. Rather than fear, however, the disciples are told to trust the Spirit for what to say, and that this will be a time to "bear testimony" (21:13). Thus witness to Christ will take place in the context of threat and persecution. That is the way it is, given this world's bent on exploiting its power and resisting justice. Still, the promise is made that "by your endurance you will gain your lives" (21:19).

Thus Jesus' life and the life of his people cannot avoid the cost of loyalty to God and God's will. Mission involves suffering, rejection, and pain. The way to the promised glory is through dying to self and living for Christ (9:23-27). Nevertheless, the promises and joy outweigh the cost, for the end is abundant life here and in the coming kingdom.

Jesus' Coming: A Light to the Nations

The programmatic sermon in Nazareth also points to a third feature in Jesus' mission, its universality. The Jewish audience in the synagogue is enraged when Jesus recalls two prophetic instances where the rejection of a prophet led to a mission outside Israel, including hated Syria. This pattern of rejection by Israel and mission to Gentiles is basic in Luke-Acts. Yet it should not be misunderstood as a rejection of Israel, or as a denial of historic Israel as a people of God. In fact, recent commentators have argued that for Luke the church is essentially restored Israel. It is the community in which God's promises to Israel are fulfilled and the hope of Israel continued. Nevertheless, it is true that in the course of history, the rejection of Jesus as Messiah at the beginning of the church's life was fundamental in the movement from Jew to Gentile. Luke makes this abundantly clear both in the Gospel and, even more, in Acts. Only a remnant of Israel came to faith, while it was the proselytes and God-fearers of the Gentile world who responded. This was a profound mystery for the early church. Luke was utterly convinced that this was all in the purpose of God, the strange way by which God in Christ willed to embrace the world. Therefore Luke, as one Gentile writing to another, tells the story of Jesus as good news for the whole world, Jew and Gentile alike.

The universality of Jesus' mission appears even in the birth narratives. While steeped in Jewish piety of the best kind, and expressing joy at God's promises to Israel now fulfilled, there is also a strong note of God's salvific plan for the world. The angels announce ". . .and on earth peace among men with whom he is pleased!" (2:14). Righteous Simeon, filled with the Spirit, prophesies that the child will be "a light for revelation to the Gentiles, and for glory to thy people Israel" (2:32). Most fascinating, Luke's stress on the historical events and characters involved in Jesus' birth is very likely his way of saying that in Jesus God is revealing himself as the true ruler and benefactor of the universe. Though Rome will put him to death, it will not defeat his rule.

Within the Gospel itself, we can point only to several main evidences of the universal purpose of God's salvation in Christ. The quotation from Isaiah introducing the Baptist's ministry adds the phrase "all flesh shall see the salvation of God" (3:4-6). During his teaching ministry, Jesus makes a special effort to include Samaritans within God's realm (10:25-37). A Roman centurion in Capernaum, a devout God-fearer, becomes a model for a faith such as is found "not even in Israel" (Luke 7:9; cf. Cornelius in Acts 10) and another centurion at the cross makes the confession of Jesus' innocence (Luke 23:47). Luke's intent becomes most clear in the authoritative teaching of the risen Lord to his disciples at the close of the Gospel (24:44-48). These words are farewell instructions for his chosen witnesses, and should be studied carefully. After revealing the scriptural testimony now fulfilled in the Messiah's death and resurrection, the command is given to preach "repentance and forgiveness of sins. . .to all nations, beginning from Jerusalem" (Luke 24:47; cf. Acts 1:8). There is no doubt that the mission is to the world: from Jerusalem to Rome to the ends of the earth. And the disciples are the called and chosen and trained witnesses to be God's instrument of redemption. When the promised Spirit comes, they will be on the march. The way is now prepared for the continuing story of the church of Jesus Christ in Acts.

In summary, for Luke history and mission go together. The salvation history consummated in Christ is the foundation for the church's mission. We have sketched three facets of this foundational history in Jesus' earthly life and ministry: his mission of good news to the poor and disenfranchised; his path through suffering to glory; and the universal embrace of his mission. Each of these provides much food for thought in terms of the church's continuing mission to the world. Jesus' life and ministry, in a powerful and irreplaceable way, is both the source and the model for our life as disciples in the present. The Lukan portrait is not dead history, but a narrative of "the things which have been accomplished among us," meant to confirm and encourage our mandate for mission in every age.

Continuing History: The Mission of the Church in Acts

In his second volume, Luke outlines his understanding of the ongoing mission of Christ in the world. What Jesus "began to do and teach, until the day when he was taken up" (Acts 1:1-2) is now continued in the life and activity of his community of followers, the people of "the way." This is an exciting story, told with the skill of a fine writer, and the passion of one who has seen the hand of God at work in history. Eyewitness or not, Luke records things in a fresh and exciting way, so that Acts has inspired believers throughout history to emulate "these first formative years."

Transitional Events

The opening chapters of Acts form the link, both historically and theologically, between the mission of Jesus and the mission of the church. Observe these three linkages. The Ascension scene provides the overall perspective (1:6-11). In contrast to the disciples' misunderstanding about the nature of the kingdom as a political-religious entity and their speculation about the time of its coming, Jesus offers a new vision of their task. They are called to be his "witnesses in Jerusalem and in all Judea and Samaria and to the end of the earth"

(1:8). This is Luke's programmatic outline of the missionary task in Acts. The power to witness will come from the Holy Spirit, who will teach them how and what to say. As for when the kingdom will come in its fullness, that is not the essential question. Their task is not to stare into heaven, but to witness in the power of the Spirit.

A second link has to do with the apostolic witness. Jesus is gone, but Luke goes to great lengths to show the vital connection that exists between the story of Jesus and the life of the church. Jesus' ministry and its redemptive meaning for humanity takes life in the apostolic preaching and teaching. The apostles qualify as called and chosen eyewitnesses of Jesus, and as witnesses of his resurrection. Their testimony is therefore the apostolic foundation upon which the church is built. Jesus is present in their preaching and teaching, and in the community founded upon it. Because of their irreplaceable importance, Luke recalls the story of Matthias's replacement of Judas in the circle of the Twelve. Soon the church itself becomes the bearer of the apostolic witness to Jesus, but its beginnings are here. In this sense, Luke agrees with Ephesians that the church is built on the foundation of apostles and prophets, with Christ Jesus the chief cornerstone (Eph. 2:20).

Of unique importance is the third key event, Pentecost. At the close of the Gospel, Jesus had instructed his disciples to wait for "the promise of [the] Father," until they are "clothed with power from on high" (24:49). This promise of empowerment by the Spirit is fulfilled on Pentecost. As Luke understands it, the outpouring of the Spirit marks the inbreaking of the promised new age (Joel 2:16-21). It is the "last days," when the Spirit is poured out on "all flesh," and "your sons and daughters shall prophesy. . .yea, and on my manservants and maidservants in those days I will pour out my Spirit." Note how Luke stresses the universality of the Spirit's gift ("*all* flesh") and its impartation to men and women alike. The long list of persons from "all nations under heaven" also gives emphasis to the universal scope of the church's new mission. Even though it takes time for the reality to sink in and requires a special revelation to Peter, the church is now set on its course of redemptive activity on behalf of the whole human race. A new missionary movement is born, with a message about Jesus of Nazareth, the crucified and risen Lord. And it is the Spirit that inspires and empowers and guides this new movement in human history, a movement destined in the plan of God to encompass the world with God's message of reconciliation and hope in Christ. It is not too much to say that for Luke, the story of the church is the story of the acts of the Holy Spirit at work in the church.

The Apostolic Preaching

Already on Pentecost, the apostles through Peter began to fulfill Jesus' command to witness. Their testimony met with open hearts, and the missionary community was on its way from Jerusalem to the ends of the earth. As Luke tells the story, the apostles played a leading role in the preaching and teaching ministry of the word (6:4). In particular, Luke narrates the witness of Peter in the first half of Acts, and Paul in the second half. Only a few other apostles are mentioned by name (John, James). Instead—and this is significant—the witnesses in the early church are mainly new converts, some of them named, but many of them forever nameless. Among those names are the seven Greek-speaking deacons, two of whom turn out to be effective evangelists (Stephen and Philip). Women are also included (Dorcas, Tabitha, Lydia), so that the net effect in Acts is a two-level kind of witnessing—the apostolic ministry which forms the vital link between Jesus and the post-resurrection community, and the ministry of all others who come to faith. Roles and functions may differ, and the priority of apostolic leadership maintained, but in effect the church is one community of faith and witness. In this sense, no one is excluded from Jesus' command, "You are my witnesses."

What is the content of the witness? Most of the time Luke is preoccupied with telling the various stories about the church's Spirit-empowered advance in the world. Once in a while he pauses to fill in the reader about what they preached and taught. These reflections are preserved especially in the famous sermons of Peter and Paul. Much work has been done investigating their content and form, and the best conclusion seems to be that they represent early Christian missionary preaching—first among Jews (Acts 2; 4; 13), and then among Gentiles (Acts 14; 17). In the early sermons we catch fresh, possibly primitive images of Jesus: servant (4:27; 3:26), man appointed by God (2:22), author of life, Holy and Righteous One (3:14). While there are differences, there is also a remarkable unity, and this is particularly true in the core kerygma (proclamation). Each one centers on Jesus as the fulfillment of promise (hence the Old Testament proof texts), and on Jesus' death and resurrection as the primary acts that attest Jesus' role as Messiah and Lord. While Acts does not stress the redemptive meaning of Jesus' death, it does unmistakably proclaim him as Savior of the world, the only "name under heaven. . . by which we must be saved" (4:12).

In the later Hellenistic sermons to Gentile pagans (Acts 14; 17), a different approach is necessary, since they have no Old Testament or Jewish background. Hence we find examples of Paul and Barnabas proclaiming knowledge of the living God who created the world and the whole human race, and of Jesus as the one by whom the world must be judged. A new audience required new approaches, and the early church responded as needed.

Thus, witness is the task laid upon the whole church, apostles and ordinary believers alike, and the message is essentially the same. The witnesses attempt in ever new and fresh ways to present Jesus as the one through whom the knowledge of God and God's forgiving love are revealed to the human race.

The Apostolic Community

Luke also provides us with brief descriptions of the early Christian community. These are tantalizing glimpses, which we would like to see more fully described. The best of these are found in the summary statements of Acts 2:42-47 and 4:32-37. Here we find a community characterized by their devotion to the apostles' teaching, the fellowship, the breaking of bread, and the prayers (2:42). Each of these four is significant and describes the core elements of Christian fellowship in every age. The result of this spiritual fellowship was a remarkable sense of unity, of joy, and of caring for one another. In fact, the surprising part of Luke's description, which all too often gets ignored as a "noble experiment that failed," is the material care for one another, the radical sharing and distributing of food with the result that no poor existed among them (4:32-35). There is both a spiritual and material unity in this community, so that they are truly bound together in faith and love for one another. Consequently, they attract increasing numbers and the word gets out to others about the new kind of community these followers of Jesus have formed (2:46-47). Far from being "a noble experiment that failed," Luke intends his description of the early church to be a model or ideal type for subsequent generations. While this does not mean a literal slavery to his description, it does show the inner dynamic at work in Spirit-created communities, and challenges each community to the same kind of spiritual and economic unity and love.

The Apostolic Mission to the World

In the remainder of this study we want to lift up four aspects of the Lukan story in Acts that focus on mission. What we say presupposes two fundamental elements of Luke's vision, namely, that the gospel mandates a universal mission to Jew and Gentile, and that this global mission is in reality the work of the risen Christ in his community through the Spirit. For the followers of Jesus of Nazareth in Galilee to envision a global task was no small task. It took them a little time, but by the second half of Acts, especially after Cornelius's conversion, there is no doubt what God had in mind. They argue yet at the Jerusalem Council about how the Gentiles will participate (Acts 15), but from then on the principle is established that Christ is offered "without the law" to the world. Christianity has always been a missionary movement embracing the whole of humanity, a spreading flame, as one historian called it. The source and power of the movement in history has always been communities and individuals of faith through whom the Spirit works. The continuing story is the Spirit's story of shaping and moving God's people in every age.

What are some specific aspects of the church's mission emphasized in Acts?

1. A reliance on prayer. Perhaps this seems a bit spiritual, given our do-it-yourself mentality. Nevertheless, one is struck by the number of times in key situations that the church or one of its leaders resorts to prayer. When the early church is under threat in Jerusalem, it gathers to pray for boldness and courage, a marvelous prayer given by Luke (Acts 4:23-31). The result was the Spirit's dynamic presence. Again, Peter is in prayer and also the centurion Cornelius when the two are informed of one another in a way that leads to their crucial encounter (Acts 10:3,9). The first martyr, Stephen, has his comforting vision of the Son of man as he prays while the stones fly (Acts 7:59). And Paul is shown praying constantly for guidance at key moments on his missionary campaigns (Acts 13:2; 16:6-9; 13; etc.). The point is clear that the church which seeks to do mission in God's power will need to be a praying church, keeping the channels open to Christ's power and guidance in whatever it does.

2. *Boldness to witness.* As the story unfolds in Acts, it quickly becomes apparent that "followers of the way" will meet with hostility and opposition and even threat of life. Hence the need for boldness, both in taking the step of "confessing" Jesus as Messiah and Lord, and in maintaining that confession. Very quickly Peter and John are arrested by the authorities and told not to speak or teach again in the name of Jesus (4:18). The authorities, however, have already observed the boldness of Peter and John (4:13) and the story ends with the two replying to their accusers, "we must obey God rather than men" (5:29). This becomes the principle throughout Acts, a boldness even at risk of life and family, out of loyalty to the Lordship of Christ (cf. 2:29; 4:9,13; 13:46; 18:26). In Acts we see fulfilled what Jesus had promised in the Gospel about testifying before kings and governors for his name's sake, and of the promise that he will provide the strength and wisdom to speak (Luke 21:12-19). So, a kind of "foolish boldness," is present, a mix between human fear and holy carefreeness to speak and act for Christ's cause, all because of the confidence that Christ is with them and that loyalty to him and his cause will not be denied. Read Stephen's speech in this light of "foolish boldness" (chap. 7), or read the encouraging word to Paul near the end of his life (23:11). This, of course, takes faith and prayer. It involves counting the cost. Yet, to be on God's side is not a bad choice in the end.

3. *The willingness to suffer.* We earlier noted how Luke in the Gospel presents Jesus' way as a movement through suffering to glory. This theme is continued in Acts. The name of Jesus, though a word of grace and peace and love, meets with resistance from ignorant and fearful persons, especially those in positions of influence. The Jewish leaders perceive the early believers as traitors to Judaism and as potential threats to their tradition and customs. They oppose the apostles in Jerusalem and Judea, and are constant troublemakers for Christian missionaries throughout the scattered cities of the empire. Synagogue visits become conflict situations, and usually result in expulsion of the

missionaries. The Roman authorities are also persecutors, but they are caught in the middle and do not appear as consistent opponents of the church. Wherever the gospel is preached, there one inevitably faces hostility. It goes with confessing Jesus, and living according to his will. So the apostles are imprisoned, Stephen and James martyred, Paul oft-stoned and whipped and in prison and on trial. Commentators have in fact noted how Luke seems to draw deliberate parallels between Jesus' journey to suffering and death and Paul's journey to Rome and imprisonment. As Jesus, so his followers. So Stephen prays the same prayer as his Lord, "Father forgive them," and sees the heavens open to receive him with the Son of man standing in greeting (7:58-59). The church on earth, the church militant, is in a conflict with evil personified in historical persons and institutions. Luke allows no glory road without the cross. Yet the promise of redemption to come, and joy and peace and boldness now, support the faithful on the way.

4. The church's potentially subversive attitude to the state. For a long time, numerous interpreters argued that Luke had written Acts at least in part as a Roman apologia. By this they meant that Luke was trying to show that Christianity was not a movement dangerous to the Roman empire. Its followers were responsible citizens, who prayed for their kings and rulers. Whatever trouble occurred with political authorities, so this theory ran, was the result of false accusations from Jewish leaders and the synagogue. Thus Luke portrays the Roman authorities as essentially respecting Paul's Roman citizenship, and consistently declaring Paul and other Christians as innocent of any political subversion. While there is some truth in this portrayal, it is not the full story. It is true that Christians in Acts are not political revolutionaries working deliberately against the state. Christian communities are not advocates of violence or hatred toward the powers that be, and the political authority of Rome is respected. It is also true that Luke may tend to exaggerate the guilt of the Jewish community in causing trouble, due to the rivalry between church and synagogue. Yet Luke makes it unmistakably clear that Christians obey God, not any ruler, including Caesar. That in itself sets them on a collision course with Rome's imperial claims. Even more, the values preached and lived by the followers of Jesus bring on them the same hostility as it did their Lord. They are "turning the world upside down" (cf. Acts 17:6) by their insistence on God's concern for the poor, suffering, and lowly of this world. They are modeling a new kind of community in which the values of justice and love challenge the old values of power and control. These Christians are bound and determined to let no lesser allegiance get in the way of their allegiance to Christ. They stubbornly and boldly confess knowledge of the one God and the person through whom God chose to reveal himself. By pointing to the cross and suffering love as the way of faith and obedience, they provoke both contempt and hatred from the powers that be, and the society around them. Thus Luke's picture is not of peaceful coexistence between church and state, but of tension, in which the followers of Christ are always seen as potentially subversive subjects because of their loyalty to Christ. Uncomfortable as this is, it is their lot in life to call no one Lord but Christ and to question every political and social and economic structure as something imperfect and in need of change. So this political agenda of Acts is part of the mission of Christ's church in the world.

Summary

Acts conveys the continuing history and mission of Christ in the world. The apostles form the link between Christ and the church. The apostolic preaching centers on Christ and the redemptive nature of his coming, and calls persons to faith. The whole church witnesses to this saving event. The apostolic community forms a model of what Christian fellowship is like, both in its devotion to apostolic preaching and its economic concern. And the apostolic mission to the world, through the power of the Spirit, embraces all of humanity, to the ends of the earth. Among its characteristics for mission are reliance on prayer, boldness to witness, willingness to suffer, and potentially subversive attitudes toward the state. Luke's story has but one aim: "You shall receive power when the Holy Spirit has come upon you; and you shall be my witnesses. . . to the end of the earth" (Acts 1:8).

3

PAUL: JUSTIFICATION AND MISSION

Roy A. Harrisville

Reasons for Mission

In the 19th century, the first theological professor to occupy a "chair" in missions in Germany gave six reasons for carrying on missionary activity in the world: dogmatic, ethical, biblical, ecclesiastical, historical, and ethnological. There are still as many and more reasons advanced today. One is that mission is grounded and established in the event of Jesus Christ and in the task of proclaiming that event to the world. But is that event itself without any direct relation to the world? Is mission required to mediate that relation?

A further reason for mission is the "expansion" of Christianity throughout a world of "darkness." Anglo-Saxon and German missionary activities were long engined by the dream of a *corpus Christianum* (i.e., a "Christendom"), and beneath that notion was the assumption of the essentially Christian character of the West. When, on August 4, 1914, 93 intellectuals published a "Manifest" in favor of the expansionist policies of Emperor Friedrich Wilhelm II—among them the most celebrated theologians of the age—they assumed the identity in aim of church and state: to "westernize," thus to "Christianize" the world. Making the world "safe for democracy" was only a secular variation on the same theme. But have not our experiences with that identification been too bitter to allow us to pursue it any longer?

A third reason for mission, particularly among Gentiles, is located in the rejection of Jesus of Nazareth as Messiah by the larger part of the synagogue: "Behold, we turn to the Gentiles" (Acts 13:46). But is mission conditioned by the historical catastrophe of Israel's rejection? And is the unbelief of the synagogue without significance for mission?

Still another reason given is that "the gospel must first be preached to all nations" (Mark 13:10)—"first" presumably establishing mission as the condition for Christ's return. But can mission be viewed exclusively from the perspective of Christ's return as future? Has that return no actual connection with the present?

Or perhaps the reason for mission is to propagandize, to proselytize, to "transplant" the church? But if so, what is the essential difference between institutional Christianity and its religious competitors? Do they not all aim at reproduction of the self? The judgment of Jesus on such self-reproduction in propagandizing or proselytizing is harsh:

> You traverse sea and land to make a single proselyte, and when he becomes a proselyte, you make him twice as much a child of hell as yourselves.
>
> (Matt. 23:15)

And as for "transplanting," is mission ended as soon as the hierarchy has taken its seat?

Finally, one current popular reason given for mission is that of bettering, humanizing the world, ridding it of its demons. No doubt, with Jesus Christ a humanizing element has been let loose in human history. But cannot inhuman powers appear in human structures and alter the face of the world for the worse? Cannot the process of ridding the world of its demons be perverted into enslavement to sacrallike powers? How can such betterment withstand the absolutizing of ideologies or theories?

Paul and the Righteousness of God

For some hint or clue as to the way out of the dilemma posed by each of these reasons for mission, we turn to the apostle, specifically to his concept of righteousness or justification.

For years it has been customary to construe Paul's concept of the righteousness of God as touching only individual existence. No one can deny that for Paul God's righteousness is of towering significance for the life of the individual. By placing exclusive accent upon righteousness as God's gracious activity toward the sinner, however, an essential component in the concept has been neglected, and it is that component which may assist us in a proper estimate of mission.

To begin with, Paul's concept of the righteousness of God has its antecedents, not only in the Christian community which preceded him and from which he drew, but also in that religion of covenant and law which he had inherited. The Hebrew term translated "righteousness" in our English Bible is best translated "community faithfulness," that is, fidelity within the relationship established by Yahweh with the people. This definition expresses the peculiar concretion which the Old Testament gives to a term whose roots reach back to ancient Canaan. But the interpretation of the term best suited to its *use* in the Old Testament is that of adherence to a norm, to an ordering of the world resting in God and sustained by God. For example, in Isaiah 45, Yahweh summons the "survivors of the nations" (v. 20) to answer, Who else but God has suited deed to word? and concludes:

> I am God, and there is no other.
> By myself I have sworn,
>   from my mouth has gone forth in righteousness
>   a word that shall not return:
> "To me every knee shall bow,
>   every tongue shall swear."
> Only in the Lord, it shall be said of me,
>   are righteousness and strength. . . .
>
> (Isa. 45:22-24)

The summons is preceded by these words:

> For thus says the Lord,
> who created the heavens
>   (he is God!),
> who formed the earth and made it
>   (he established it;
> he did not create it a chaos,

he formed it to be inhabited!):
"I am the Lord, and there is no other. . . ."

(Isa. 45:18)

The God who created the earth a cosmos, an ordered world, is the One who "speaks the truth" (i.e., speaks "righteousness"). God's salvation is the consequence of God's creation of the world, and thus both creation and salvation belong to God's righteousness.

The example from Second Isaiah is not at all unique. The same link between God's arrangement of the world and God's saving activity, forged in God's righteousness, is a recurring theme in the Old Testament. The presupposition beneath the ritual laws in the Pentateuch is that sinful existence consists in a wrongful relationship to the order or arrangement built into the fabric of the world created by God. For this reason we encounter the innumerable prohibitions in Leviticus and Numbers respecting not merely internal states, but also the material world and thus the body—that portion of the material world for which the individual is most directly responsible. From this perspective also, the great cultic festival, the Day of Atonement, emerges as the creating and liberating activity of God by which the world, fallen away from its Creator, is newly shaped and established. The conclusion of a modern service for Yom Kippur reads:

> Now, therefore, O Lord our God, impose thine awe upon all thy works, and thy dread upon all that thou hast created, that all works may fear thee and all creatures prostrate themselves before thee, that they may all form a single hand to do thy will with a perfect heart. . . . Holy art thou, and dreaded is thy name, and there is no God beside thee, as it is written, And the Lord of hosts is exalted in judgment, and the holy God is sanctified in righteousness.[1]

This link between creation, salvation, or deliverance and the righteousness of God has its echo in literature outside the Old Testament. In "The Book of Mysteries" from Qumran, "righteousness" is identified with "the norm of the world":

> When the children of Perversity are shut up, then Wickedness shall retire before Righteousness as [da]rkness retires before the Light, and as smoke

vanishes and [is] no more, so shall Wickedness vanish for ever and Righteousness appear like the sun, the norm of the world.[2]

A further aspect of this concept of creation and deliverance as sprung from righteousness appears in the description of the agent of God's creative and liberating activity in the so-called wisdom literature of the Jewish community:

> The Lord by wisdom founded the earth;
> by understanding he established the heavens;
> by his knowledge the deeps broke forth,
> and the clouds drop down the dew.
>
> (Prov. 3:19-20)

Of equal importance is the identification of Wisdom with worship and Law, with cultus and Torah:

> The one who created me [i.e., Wisdom] assigned a place
> for my tent.
> And he said, "Make your dwelling in Jacob,
> and in Israel receive your inheritance."
> . . . In the holy tabernacle I ministered before him,
> and so I was established in Zion.
> In the beloved city likewise he gave me a resting place,
> and in Jerusalem was my dominion.
>
> (Sirach 24:8,10-11)

> [Wisdom] is the book of the commandments of God,
> and the law that endures for ever.
> All who hold her fast will live,
> and those who forsake her will die.
>
> (Bar. 4:1)

Thus, "community faithfulness," righteousness, fidelity to the order and harmony of the world means to revere the habitation and "laws" of the Agent by which God not only first created and fixed the world, but also saves it, restores its order and harmony:

> Who hast learned thy counsel,
> unless thou hast given wisdom

> and sent thy holy Spirit from on high?
> And thus the paths of those on earth were set right,
> and men were taught what pleases thee,
> and were saved by wisdom.
>
> (Wis. 9:17-18)

Within this Jewish complex of tradition, in the context of the creating and liberating activity of God as mediated by God's Wisdom, Paul's theme of the righteousness of God is set.

For Paul, of course, everything hinges upon the precise definition of that agency by which God creates and redeems. He is not content with hypostasizing, with assigning personality to some attribute of Deity and letting the matter rest there. He identifies the Wisdom of God with the concrete, historical person Jesus, whom he came to acknowledge as the Christ. Christ, then, is the "wisdom of God" (1 Cor. 1:24,30; 2:6-7); he is the "likeness" or, better, "the image of God"—a term clearly calculated to link Christ to the activity of God in creation (2 Cor. 4:4-5); Christ is Mediator of all creation:

> For us there is one God, the Father, from whom are all things, and for whom we exist, and one Lord, Jesus Christ, through whom are all things and through whom we exist.
>
> (1 Cor. 8:6)

The language and conceptuality of Paul are equal with that of the ancient sage: Wisdom, "all-powerful, overseeing all, and penetrating through all spirits that are intelligent and pure and most subtle." Wisdom "pervades and penetrates all things." She is "breath of the power of God, and a pure emanation of the glory of the Almighty." She is a "reflection of eternal light, a spotless mirror of the working of God, and an image of his goodness." "While remaining in herself," wisdom—"initiate in the knowledge of God, and an associate in his works"—"renews all things" (Wis. 7:23-27; 8:4; cf. chaps. 7–9 passim). In Paul, however, that language and conceptuality are warped to the shape of Jesus proclaimed as Lord.

Further, in contrast to the secrecy surrounding the encounter between God and God's creatures in the temple's Holy of Holies—Wisdom's "dwelling" (Sir. 24:8-9)—and in contrast with that encounter itself which could only occur in figure or parable (the second temple lacked both ark and *kaphoreth,* "mercy-seat"), Paul writes that God has broken the silence, publicly set Jesus forth, made his death of expiatory effect—and all in order to "show" God's righteousness, to prove that he is creator and renewer of the earth:

> [Him] God put forward as an expiation by his blood, to be received by faith. This was to show God's righteousness, because in his divine forbearance he had passed over former sins; it was to prove at the present time that he himself is righteous and that he justifies him who has faith in Jesus.
>
> (Rom. 3:25-26)

> For our sake he made him to be sin who knew no sin, so that in him we might become the righteousness of God.
>
> (2 Cor. 5:21)

In these texts, the apostle is citing formulas already in existence prior to his own coming to faith, but he shapes the tradition into a massive critique of Mosaic Law. Since by raising Jesus from the dead, God had identified himself with the One cursed by the Law (Deut. 21:22-23), had made him the embodiment of his righteousness, that righteousness has been revealed "apart from law" (Rom. 3:21). Now, obedience to the "norm of the world" cannot be achieved through an existence arranged according to judicial decree, but is a gift from God—"by faith" (Rom. 1:16-17). But "by faith" spells not merely atonement, but participation in righteousness itself, in the very life of God who creates and redeems. Thus Paul writes:

> [God] is the source of your life in Christ Jesus, whom God made our wisdom, our righteousness and sanctification and redemption.
>
> (1 Cor. 1:30)

We expand our earlier conclusion respecting the context of Paul's theme of righteousness to read that *within the complex of the Jewish tradition of the creating and liberating activity of God—but in contrast to that tradition as it is mediated through Jesus Christ, God's "Wisdom"—Paul's theme of righteousness is set.*

There is more. Paul's understanding of the righteousness of God reaches beyond earliest Christian tradition. If for Paul faith spells participation in righteousness, in the creating and redeeming activity of God; if it spells existence "in Christ"; then existence by faith is characterized by a dynamic, an intrinsic energy, by an unresting hasting toward a goal, since the righteousness of God, that creating and saving activity of God, is intent on winning back and restoring everything God has made. This is what Paul means when he describes Christian existence as new, or addresses the company of believers as the "new creation":

> Therefore, if any one is in Christ, he is a new creation; the old has passed away, behold, the new has come.
>
> (2 Cor. 5:17)

> For neither circumcision counts for anything, nor uncircumcision, but a new creation.
>
> (Gal. 6:15)

The references in Paul to faith in Christ, to life in righteousness as a new existence, are legion. And over it all—over this righteousness of God, this restless, dynamic activity of God toward the world; over the existence of those who are caught up into this activity by faith, over this "new creation"—Paul writes the word "Spirit":

> The law of the Spirit of life in Christ Jesus has set me free from the law of sin and death. . . .To set the mind on the Spirit is life and peace. . . . He who raised Christ Jesus from the dead will give life to your mortal bodies also through his Spirit. . . .When we cry, "Abba! Father!" it is the Spirit himself bearing witness with our spirit that we are children of God, . . .heirs of God and fellow heirs with Christ. . . .We know that the whole creation has been groaning in travail together until now; and not only the creation, but we ourselves, who have the first fruits of the Spirit, groan inwardly as we wait for adoption. . . .
>
> (Romans 8, passim)

Thus, the name for God's action toward the world, the name for his righteousness is "Spirit":

> For the kingdom of God is not food and drink but righteousness and peace and joy in the Holy Spirit.
>
> (Rom. 14:17)

> Now the Lord is the Spirit, and where the Spirit of the Lord is, there is freedom.
>
> (2 Cor. 3:17)

Righteousness, then, justification, far from reflecting exclusive application to the reconciliation between God and the sinner, is also far from limiting that reconciliation to one or the other person in the Godhead. It is an activity of the whole of Deity toward the totality of creation, an activity characterized by tension and a straining toward an end when God will be "everything to every one" (1 Cor. 15:28). Accordingly, our original conclusion should be further revised to read that *within the context of the Jewish tradition of the creating and liberating activity of God, but in contrast to that tradition as mediated through Jesus Christ, and beyond earliest Christian tradition as characterized by newness, by "Spirit," and thus as the activity of the entire Godhead toward the world, Paul's understanding of righteousness is set.*

It would be an error, however, to construe Paul's concept of righteousness as an activity of the entire Godhead in any speculative sense, as though he regarded "God," "Wisdom," "Christ," "newness," or "Spirit" as interchangeable, each able to "stand in" for the other. Quite the contrary—for Paul the divine righteousness had been "revealed" (cf. Rom. 1:17; 16:25; Gal. 3:23), unmasked in a concrete, palpable, historical act which engaged the conditions of this world in judgment and reconciliation. The righteousness of God had assumed flesh and temporality:

> If, because of one man's trespass, death reigned through that one man, much more will those who receive the abundance of grace and the free gift of righteousness reign in life through the one man Jesus Christ.
>
> (Rom. 5:17)

Thus, for all its cosmic dimension, the accent in Paul's concept of the righteousness of God clearly falls on the event which guarantees to that concept its creation-theological dimension, and to which his references to the new creation or the Spirit are bent, namely, the event of Jesus Christ, "born of woman, born under the law" (Gal. 4:4).

The Reasons Revisited

In light of Paul's concept of the righteousness of God, we turn to the reasons for mission indicated at the outset of the chapter:

1. Mission is not "grounded" or "established" in the event of Jesus Christ. It is rather that event itself, the activity of the Creator intent on winning back all he has made, the epiphany of God in the world. Since that epiphany is mediated through Jesus Christ, Lord of the world, that Mediator needs no further mediation ("now an intermediary implies more than one; but God is one," Gal. 3:20)—everything in the world is immediate to him:

> Therefore God has highly exalted him and bestowed on him the name which is above every name, that at the name of Jesus every knee should bow, in heaven and on earth and under the earth, and every tongue confess that Jesus Christ is Lord to the glory of God the Father.
>
> (Phil. 2:9)

For this reason, the proclamation of the event of Jesus Christ, rather than establishing the basis for mission, is itself established in the mission of God, in the revelation of his righteousness:

> All this is from God, who through Christ reconciled us to himself and gave us the ministry of reconciliation. . . . So we are ambassadors for Christ, God making his appeal through us. We beseech you on behalf of Christ, be reconciled to God.
>
> (2 Cor. 5:19-20)

2. Mission cannot be identified with the expansion of Christianity construed as a morally superior existence, aligned or not with a given nation or culture. Paul's incessant concentration upon the righteousness of God as revealed in Jesus Christ apart from the Law; his attacks on any and all who sought to modify or attenuate that theme (cf. Gal. 1:6-9); his boasting (cf. 2 Cor. 11:5-6,16-17,21-29; 12:1-4); and his summons to be imitators of him (cf. Phil. 3:17) might all be set down to an incredible egotism, if it did not throb with the conviction that he was not worth the grace or the task given to him:

> For I am the least of the apostles, unfit to be called an apostle, because I persecuted the church of God. But by the grace of God I am what I am, and his grace toward me was not in vain.
>
> (1 Cor. 15:9-10)

For Paul, access to righteousness occurred without previous performance, from out of God's unsearchable and incomprehensible grace for the sake of Christ who as Lord had accepted him and sustained him in faith. For this reason, the apostle's apparent preening and call to imitation were ultimately only a summons to "boast in the Lord," since he regarded himself as nothing. The apostle would scarcely have agreed with an Adolf von Harnack, who wrote that the atmosphere from which the chief ingredients in earliest Christian preaching derived their vitality was the absolute supremacy of the "moral element." As Paul himself wrote:

> I planted, Apollos watered, but God gave the growth. So neither he who plants nor he who waters is anything, but only God who gives the growth. (1 Cor. 3:6-7)

3. The mission of God among the Gentiles is not the consequence of the synagogue's rejection of Jesus as Messiah. The direct result of its rejection was the Messiah's death on the cross, by which God deals with the entire world. Since the mission of God necessarily included the entire cosmos, what was at stake was Israel's obedience to a righteousness witnessed in "the law and the prophets" (Rom. 3:21). Israel's unauthorized anticipation of the gathering of the nations—a "mission reserved to God for the end-time now broken in, its attempt to establish righteousness through observance of judicial decree (Rom. 9:31-33; 10:3), its rejection of the gospel "first" addressed to it (Rom. 1:17)—these in the end spelled Israel's rejection of itself. But despite all, the righteousness of God has not passed Israel by. Israel remains the object of God's creating and liberating activity—"for the gifts and call of God are irrevocable" (Rom. 11:29). Mission, then, apostleship among the Gentiles, far from the result of Israel's rejection, is precisely the occasion for Israel's coming to faith (Rom. 11:13-15): "To the Jew first and also to the Greek"—to enable mission to the Jew again (cf. Rom. 11:25, 31-32).

4. Mission is not the condition for Christ's return. Mission is itself of a piece with the end-time. It is the gathering of the nations already begun and certain to be completed. The tension within which mission is set, therefore, is not a tension between present and future, as though

the time between Christ's cross and his return could be abstracted or schematized. The tension in which mission is set inheres in the nature of righteousness itself, by which God is at work to embrace the whole world. Not even the popular description of God's righteousness, as manifest "now already" but "not yet" brought to its fulfillment, is adequate to its definition. Or again, the fact that on one occasion Paul can write to the Corinthians, "But you were washed, you were sanctified, you were justified in the name of the Lord Jesus Christ and in the Spirit of our God" (1 Cor. 6:11), or on still another write that "through the Spirit, by faith, we wait for the hope of righteousness" (Gal. 6:6), does not spell imperfection in righteousness, a contrast between what is and what ought to be, the distance between the two somehow needing to be bridged. Then tension within the righteousness of God springs from its nature as a centrifugal force, a "newness" inexorably thrusting out to embrace its object—"every knee" and "every tongue." For this reason, the apostle is so incredibly sanguine in the issuing of summonses, imperatives, and exhortations to his readers. It is inevitable that God will have his way:

> Do not yield your members to sin as instruments of wickedness, but yield yourselves to God as men who have been brought from death to life, and your members to God as instruments of righteousness. For sin will have no dominion over you.
>
> (Rom. 6:13-14)

5. The mission of the church is not the mission of God. Identification of God's creating and liberating activity of the entire cosmos with the transplanting or establishment of the church limits the scope of that activity and abstracts the existence of the church from it. The mission of the church can only share in the all-encompassing righteousness of God, and only in this sense be called the mission of God. For this reason, the church is not the "citadel of faith," carrying on its existence apart from actual, empirical life, but rather is the place at which the world may "breathe" the righteousness of God:

> Thanks be to God, who in Christ always leads us in triumph, and through us spreads the fragrance of the knowledge of him everywhere. For we are the aroma of Christ to God.
>
> (2 Cor. 2:14-15)

Not even an apostle could lay claim to independent existence. "Grace and apostleship" were something Paul had "received" (Rom. 1:5), and "not from men nor through man," but from God who "was pleased to reveal his Son" to him (Gal. 1:1,16). Moreover, the apostle conceived his mission of announcing the righteousness of God in Christ as dependent upon the body to which he belonged, even upon congregations he had not founded:

> I thank my God through Jesus Christ for all of you, because your faith is proclaimed in all the world. . . . I long to see you, that I may impart to you some spiritual gift to strengthen you, that is, that we may be mutually encouraged by each other's faith, both yours and mine.
>
> (Rom. 1:8-12)

More important still, that body to which Paul and his fellow sharers in God's mission belonged, had itself come into existence only through the activity of God:

> For by one Spirit we were all baptized into one body—Jews or Greeks, slaves or free—and all were made to drink of one Spirit.
>
> (1 Cor. 12:13)

The mission of the church is not the mission of God. The mission of God is the mission of the church.

6. Finally, the orientation of God's righteousness is not toward the alteration of conditions or relationships in this world which allows the self to remain unaltered or unchanged. It is rather oriented toward the alteration of the self in which the world as it exists is incorporated, to the justification and renewal of the sinner which frees the sinner for penetration of that deadly circle of mere intrahuman encounter. Where men and women are sustained at the center of their existence by the creating and liberating activity of God, they are able to withstand the absolutizing of ideologies and the danger of massive mediocrity. Where the person is embraced through faith by the righteousness of God, the other, the neighbor and the neighbor's need, can become regulative of action. As Christ emerged from out of his true and authentic existence to live and to die among sinners, the partisans of God's righteousness

live for the world. But there can be life for the world only where the self has died and been raised for the world:

> I appeal to you therefore, brethren, by the mercies of God, to present your bodies as a living sacrifice, holy and acceptable to God, which is your spiritual worship. Do not be conformed to this world but be transformed by the renewal of your mind, that you may prove what is the will of God, what is good and acceptable and perfect.
>
> (Rom. 12:1-2)

4

CHRIST AND MISSION: THE FOURTH GOSPEL AND OUR WITNESS

Merlin H. Hoops

The Fourth Gospel is a fascinating object of study—because of the manner in which it is composed, the context which it reflects, and the Christological focus of its message. The careful integration of these elements with distinctive symbols aids the evangelist in presenting a Gospel with a well-defined but general purpose: "Now Jesus did many other signs. . ., but these are written that you may believe that Jesus is the Christ, the Son of God" (20:30-31).

The stated purpose suggests an intent to persuade. Persuade in which sense? This question has long plagued Johannine scholars. This question arises because of the ambiguity of some words in the stated purpose: "written *that you may believe*" (20:30a).[1] Is this a reference to confirming the believer in his or her faith? Is this clause a reference to confronting the nonbeliever with persuasive mission propaganda?[2] The ambiguity in this statement is probably one reason why Raymond Brown defines this Gospel's purpose as he does: "This is a gospel designed to root the believer deeper in his faith. The stated purpose of the gospel in 20:30 is probably not primarily missionary.[3]

The ambiguity of the evangelist's description of purpose and the lack of explicit mission statements elsewhere in the Gospel have made the subject of mission in the Fourth Gospel a controversial one.[4] Nevertheless, the popular premise that the mission task was not in dispute for the first-century church[5] has led scholars to continue to examine this significant Gospel for indirect statements about mission.[6] It has led to commonalities in approach toward Johannine studies insofar as composition and context are regularly considered,[7] textual selections examined, and Christological thrusts explored. This is the general approach followed in this chapter. It will be presupposed that the Christological focus of the Gospel is the key to understanding much of its message.

The Fourth Gospel: Composition, Context, and Language

Our subject calls for exploring the text in its canonical form.[8] It is proper to consider the final product as the fullest expression of the Johannine tradition. But a focus on the final text does not preclude a critical awareness of the variety of influences which have given it shape.[9] A critical awareness of such influences can lead to a greater appreciation of the final shape of the composition and the traditional language it reinterprets; it can lead to a better understanding of the reason why a certain selection of texts is appropriate for a specific study of mission.

Abbreviated descriptions seldom do justice to the integrated message which confronts the reader of this Gospel. A reference to its *spiral form of argument,* however, illustrates some of its attractive and challenging aspects. Hoskyns and Davey described this Johannine characteristic decades ago:

> The fourth gospel takes the form of an almost continuous argument, which passes quite imperceptibly from narrative to explanation. . . .(It) is mainly composed of long discourses. And, quite apart from their length, they have a highly distinctive spiral form of argument.[10]

The evangelist registers a thought, contemplates it from every angle and apparently finishes up where he started. Yet, in the process there is a slight but perceptible movement.[11]

The spiral form of argument is an ideal form for the author's reinterpretation and reappropriation of traditional symbols, for his use of such symbols to make a more universalizing impact. Pheme Perkins presents a fine description of the latter process:

> We should remember that the author is often using well-established religious symbols and language in unexpected contexts and relationships. . . .Sometimes John's symbolic language serves a universalizing function. Such general symbols permit people from a wide variety of cultural contexts to appropriate the Christian revelation by seeing Christ as the fulfillment of all humanity's religious aspirations. But the way in which John reuses Old Testament and earlier Christian religious language suggests that he has an even more specific intent: to provide a new understanding of the traditional language.[12]

Perhaps the spiral form of this Gospel's presentation and the reappropriation of traditional language are not of direct assistance in uncovering explicit mission teaching. Yet they surely offer insights as to its universal appeal and offer a powerful way of communicating the relevance of Christ.

And the context? It is a common conviction of recent scholarship that the community from which the Fourth Gospel originated was in dialog with a wide spectrum of groups and ideologies of the first century. Raymond Brown, for example, has suggested that the Johannine community went through a series of stages as it developed its own Christology and community identity.[13] According to Brown, the Gospel as we have it evolved over a number of years.[14]

In his own pioneering study, J. Louis Martyn has identified the decade of the 80s as the decade in which Jewish Christians were excommunicated from the synagogue.[15] He suggests that during the very first period of Christianity two types of Jews existed side by side within the synagogue. These consisted of Jews who did and those who did not believe in Jesus as the Christ. This situation of fraternal coexistence continued well into the end of the first century. As it was restructuring itself after the disastrous war with Rome, Judaism found it necessary to tighten up. Consequently, it reduced its toleration for deviant beliefs, such as the confession that Jesus was the Christ. How was the toleration reduced? The answer involves a Jewish formal prayer used in synagogue worship, the Eighteen Benedictions. Martyn, agreeing with earlier scholars, concludes that in the year A.D. 85, the 12th of these Benedictions was revised so as to exclude Christians specifically.[16]

What were the practical consequences? This new formulation was a way of detecting those Jews who desired to hold a dual allegiance to Moses and to Jesus as Messiah. Even against the will of some of the synagogue leaders, the "Benediction" regarding the heretics was now employed in order formally and finally to separate the church from the synagogue.

The event in A.D. 85 provides a context for the references to excommunication in John 9:22; 12:42; and 16:2. Additionally, it has come to be used to explain the basic twofold division of the Fourth Gospel, the first section dealing with the public ministry of Jesus and the second with the more private teaching of disciples. Donfried puts it this way: The first half, John 1–12, deals with events prior to the break with the synagogue. There is a dialog going on between those Jews who believe that Jesus is the Christ and those Jews who do not. The second half of the Gospel, John 13–20, deals with events after the break with the synagogue. The most important of these is the fact that a new Christian community exists which is in urgent need of support and guidance. Much of the second half can be viewed as a "support document" for this infant community, scarred by the break.[17]

If one accepts the preceding argument, then one can understand more fully the reason for Martyn's emphasis on a two-level approach in portions of the Gospel's presentation.[18] One can understand why many scholars continue to work with a twofold outline (chaps. 1–12, 13–20). One can understand why selections for an assessment of mission and the Fourth Gospel can be made from the first 12 chapters. This does not, of course, preclude other references (such as 17:20), including those to the resurrected Christ and his disciples. But with such a twofold sectioning of the Gospel, one can appreciate the inclusion of the more parochial "fellowship chapters" in the second major portion.

Texts for Mission: The "What" of Witness (A Gift of Love that the World not Perish)

The prolog (1:1-18) has attracted the attention of scholars through the ages. As an overture, it offers the theme music for the composition which follows. As a hymn to the Logos, it states the origin, purpose, and cosmic proportions of Jesus' mission from the Father. But other selections also set forth the message and implications of mission—for instance, two texts which appear in our common church-year lectionary, 3:14-21 and 12:20-33.[19]

Apart from the prolog, no discourse in John contains so much sheer, concentrated theology as the discourse embedded in chap. 3. With regard to the discourse in 3:2-21, Hoskyns writes that Jesus "has nothing to hide. . . . He lays bare all the fundamental themes of His mission. . . ."[20] The second selection, 12:20-33, is often seen as a great missionary text in John.[21] Both texts incorporate terminology more familiar to most modern readers than the pregnant but difficult term *Logos*.

3:14-21

An outline of this lectionary text serves to introduce and reacquaint the reader with many of the details of chap. 3. It also reminds one of the highly integrated character of the section in which the text is embedded. The text in outline:

3:14-15 A lifting up
- v. 14—The serpent of the Jewish tradition
- v. 15—The Son of man lifted up

3:16-17 A revelatory event—an act of love
- v. 16a—Son given
- v. 17a—Son sent

3:18-21 Possibilities and responses
- v. 18—Judgment and faith
- vv. 19-21—Light and darkness

The monolog within the text in question arises out of Jesus' dialog with Nicodemus.[22] In the dialog, Nicodemus's three statements and/or questions (3:2,4,9) lead Jesus to offer progressively longer responses (3:3,5,11) before he engages in monolog. But the primary focus in the exchange is the response. What is the crux of the response? It is this: Salvation is not from humans but from God.

In the dialog (3:1-10) Nicodemus is unable to grasp the idea of "being born anew." In response to his inability to grasp the idea of spiritual rebirth, Jesus offers the well-known words "Truly, truly, I say to you, unless one is born of water and the Spirit, he cannot enter the kingdom of God" (3:5).

In the continuing discussion, Jesus develops two analogies, which together explain the necessity of being born from above.[23] The first appears in 3:6: "That which is born of the flesh is flesh, and that which is born of the Spirit is Spirit." With these words, Jesus reminds the reader that this being born from above, this being born of the Spirit, is the only way a person can traverse the distance which separates the realm of God from the human condition. The "what" of our witness, of our message is made clear: Only God can lead one into the kingdom, can give eternal life.

Jesus, in the second analogy, uses the Greek word *pneuma,* which has a twofold meaning: "wind" and "spirit" (3:8). A person, he suggests, can experience the natural phenomenon of the wind. As with the wind, so with the Spirit. Just as persons hear the mysterious wind, so some will hear the sound, the voice, of the Spirit.

Jesus used common analogies in his teaching. In spite of this, Nicodemus was unable to understand. Because of this inability, he could not comprehend greater mysteries (the things of heaven) which Jesus came to reveal. Nor could he understand the confirmation of what Jesus said, a confirmation by way of the ascent/descent motif (3:13).

The dialog between Jesus and Nicodemus offers a proper background for the monolog, which continues in the selected text. Additionally, that dialog offers insights and clarifications about baptismal terminology and Baptism for contemporaries involved in witnessing, in the "mission" enterprise. It suggests that the contemporary term "born-again Christian" is not really an apt description of a person who has suddenly become very serious about Jesus the Christ. Obach and Kirk suggest that "the term 'born again Christian' is not a suitable phrase for this conversion experience." They continue: "The movement of a person from a position of merely taking Jesus for granted to a position of sincerely trying to live as God wills is, indeed, a gift for which we should pray. But the danger in referring to this conversion process as being 'born again' is that it undermines the Johannine understanding of the sacrament of Baptism."[24] John does write about a "being born anew" (3:3,5). But when he alludes to Baptism for the Christian reader, he is speaking about the movement of being an offspring of human parents to a becoming a child of God. That "being born anew," that birth from above, is accomplished only in Baptism. Therefore, only the person who is on the level of a Nicodemus can be "born again." The Christian, by definition, is one who has already been "born again."

The discussion between Jesus and Nicodemus is significant for a proper understanding of Baptism. It suggests a careful theologizing for those who study and share the "what" of witnessing. But, as suggested earlier, it also provides a backdrop for the text that follows, 3:14-21. That text provides continuing reflections, reflections which use 3:13 as a transitional point.

An incident in the book of Numbers (21:9) serves as a reference point in the so-called *hypsōthēnai* ("lifting up") passage (3:14).[25] This obscure incident is used typologically to make several points (see 3:14f.):

- As the snake was lifted up, so must Jesus be lifted up on a pole (the cross).
- As God's will was evident there, so here.
- As natural life was restored for those looking up, so eternal life is available to all who look up in faith upon the one hanging on the cross.

Through this use of an obscure incident, John asserts that the death, resurrection, and ascension of Jesus the Christ are the means through which believers can have eternal life.

The "what" of witnessing is carefully described by using the incident from Numbers. But nowhere is it as succinctly stated as in John 3:16. Here the message is so clearly expressed that it has become the one passage best known in Christendom—it is the gospel in miniature.

Four significant features in 3:16 will be given attention here:

The motivation—God's love;
The object of love—the world;
The purpose of love—eternal life;
The scope of love—"whoever."

God gave! God gave not just another teacher (3:2) but God's unique and only Son. God gave. That action in the context of this Gospel involved the gift of God's Son in incarnation (1:14) and crucifixion/exaltation (3:14). But in the immediate context, it seems that a narrower interpretation is also possible.[26] Why the latter? The choice of the word *give* provides one clue. It is unusual. This evangelist usually speaks of the Father "sending" the Son (see 3:17).[27] And later in the Gospel, there will be an emphasis on the completion of the "work" for which Jesus has been sent (see 17:4 and 19:30). The giving then, narrowly focused, includes an emphasis on the giving up in death on the cross.

God gave! That act was motivated by *agape,* a love which can best be described as a love that is all give, a love that is able to encompass the repulsive. Words from 1 John 4:10 serve as a commentary: "In this is love, not that we loved God but that he loved us and sent his Son to be the expiation for our sins."

God loved! He loved what? The world![28] This is the world of humanity, a world that includes Jews (3:1) and Samaritans (4:42) and Greeks (12:20).

God loved! What is the result? That love makes possible eternal life—for those who believe. And eternal life? That is a life of quality, a life which knows something of the serenity and peace of God. In the words of John 17:3, "this is eternal life, that they may know thee the only true God, and Jesus Christ whom thou hast sent."

God so loved the world that *whoever*. . . .The message is clear. God sent his Son into the framework of human life in order to save it, not to condemn it (3:17). But a gift sometimes presents a crisis. It does so for the world. It brings the world to a crisis in the sense that persons must choose between the light which is Jesus and the darkness which is both sin and a refusal to believe (3:19).

In the section 3:19-31 the evangelist clarifies this by using the language of dualism. Such language often oversimplifies reality, but it does reflect rather clearly what is at stake. Through such stark contrasts, individuals learn about an urgency that confronts all humanity. In such conceptualizing, there are only two life-styles. Each depends upon what is chosen. In not choosing, one sentences oneself. One continues in darkness.[29]

The significant section 3:16-21 provides many details about the "what" of our witness. It suggests that Christianity has to do with a love, a gift of love given so that the world not perish. It offers a discussion about the necessity of belief in Jesus for salvation. It suggests that the message of Christianity is a message of urgency, as offering a difference between light and darkness in this world, a world for which

Christ came. In the words of some scholars, it suggests a way to authentic existence!

12:20-33

There are numerous ways in which one can approach this significant pericope. One effective way is to focus on the major items within the text itself. As always, connections with other sections have to be taken seriously. As with chap. 3, an outline of the structure can provide an appropriate point with which to commence.

12:20-22 Introduction to the announcement of "the hour"
- v. 20—Greeks worship at the feast
- v. 21—Greeks approach Philip
- v. 22—Philip and Andrew speak to Jesus

12:23 Announcement—the hour has come

12:24-26 Collection of sayings (suffering and discipleship)
- v. 24—Miniature parable
- v. 25—Saying—loving/hating life
- v. 26—Meaning of discipleship

12:27-30 A return to the theme of glorification
- v. 27—Jesus' turmoil-hour arrives
- v. 28a—Prayer
- v. 28b—Voice
- v. 29—Two opinions—in the crowd
- v. 30—Interpretation

12:31-32 Pronouncement—passion anticipated
- v. 31—Satan destroyed
- v. 32—Many will be drawn to Jesus

12:33 The evangelist's interpretation

The spiral movement of the evangelist's presentation calls to mind various individuals and groups, even as one's attention is drawn to a new group appearing in this text. The new group! Who can ever forget those who came forth with the request, "Sir, we wish to see Jesus" (12:21)? Perhaps that request is one reason why this pericope has often been dubbed "John's missionary text."

Whatever the reaction to the Greeks' request, the Pharisees' lament in the preceding scene (12:19) seemed to be in order: "You see that you can do nothing; look, the world has gone after him." The lament was in order (from their perspective) because the Greeks, in coming to the feast, began to fulfill their fears.[30] In their own way, these Greeks symbolized the universality of Jesus' mission.

The Greeks do not personally see Jesus. But their presence at the feast with Philip is an indication to Jesus that the hour of death and glory is at hand. After that hour, after that "lifting up" on the cross, the gospel will encompass both Jew and Greek.

The incident involving the Greeks serves as a commentary (see 12:19). Additionally, it serves as a catalyst for the exposition which follows (12:23). With the statement "the hour has come," it, in fact, becomes evident that the public teaching and ministry of Jesus is coming to a close.[31]

Jesus says: "The hour has come!" He thereby draws attention to the moment when he will accomplish salvation for the world. The hour is the moment when he, the Son of man, is to be glorified upon the cross.

The coming of the hour of glorification is not a selfish groping for personal honor. On the contrary, it invites great renunciation. This renunciation is made apparent in the parable about a grain of wheat. Initially, the parable seems to interrupt the exposition. In reality, it offers an interpretation related to those in the Synoptics (cf. Mark 8:34ff.).

In the parable (12:24), attention is directed to the law of nature. In nature, death is essential for the increase of life. Since death is essential for the increase of life, the point becomes clear. Either the grain remains nothing by itself *or* it bears much fruit. The dying of the seed is then the condition for the future harvest. The productivity of the grain will be evident in the harvest of Jesus' redeeming death and resurrection.

The exposition of the parable illuminates the cross and discipleship (vv. 25-26). In plain language, living on this earth does involve priorities. Those who seek to preserve self at the expense of all other factors will perish through the destroying power of death.

> He who loves his life loses it, and he who hates his life in this world will keep it for eternal life.[32]
>
> (John 12:25)

The approach of the searching Greeks illuminates the meaning of the cross for the world. That meaning continues through the ages. But a further testimony is presented in the scene which follows (12:27-30).

The scene beginning with the words "Now is my soul troubled" (12:27a) is John's parallel to the Gethsemane scene in the Synoptics.[33] It is his parallel, yet a parallel with a difference. In the Synoptics, fear and dread are evident. Here Jesus' single-mindedness is in the forefront.

Perhaps the evangelist's unique presentation of the cross best explains the Johannine perspective regarding the agony. For John, too, the cross interprets the mission of Jesus. But in this Gospel, it is the cross that is especially the moment of revelation, because it brings about the glorification of the Father and the Son. In chap. 3, the gift of the Son (lifted up) reveals the love of the Father for humanity. In the context of chap. 12, that lifting up is also a manifestation of the love of Jesus for the world. After all, he is the Good Shepherd. As such, he lays down his life for the sheep (10:11; cf. 13:1ff.).

The fascinating message of the text continues in the concluding section (12:31-33), when it repeats some earlier pronouncements anticipating the passion. Additionally, it sounds the note of victory. Through the lifting up of this one on the cross, sin's hold on humankind has been broken. The world, which thrills in judging others, is itself judged. The Son, as the One lifted up, becomes the Savior of the world. Through the presence of Christ in Word and in the Holy Spirit, persons of all nations will be drawn again to God.[34]

In this pericope, the request "Sir, we wish to see Jesus" is given a favorable response. The search of the Greeks is not in vain. Through the lifting up on a cross, they and others will see him and discover his presence. They, and all others who look up at the cross, will have eternal life.

The powerful description of this "mission" text functions as part of the concluding section of John's presentation of Jesus' public ministry. What remains is a final word of judgment and a final call to faith. But the "what" of witnessing continues as a message for the world even as it spills over into, and permeates the life of, Christ's followers. In the message of chap. 13, after Jesus has washed the feet of disciples, he shares this challenge (13:12b-15): "He said to them, 'Do you know what I have done to you? You call me Teacher and Lord; and you are right, for so I am. If I then, your Lord and Teacher, have washed your feet, you also ought to wash one another's feet. For I have given you an example, that you also should do as I have done to you.' " And he continues that challenge in 13:34-35: "A new commandment I give to you, that you love one another; even as I have loved you, that you also love one another. By this all men will know that you are my disciples, if you have love for one another."

Can the "what" of witness ever do without an enactment of that faith in life? In this "mission" endeavor, is not the indirect witnessing of a Mother Teresa a witness in which all are to participate? Is a gospel which encompasses life ever without "mission" results, indirect though the witness may be?

Texts for Mission: The "How" of Witness (Responsibility in a Privileged Relationship)

In his recent analysis of Johannine Christology, Loader selects the reflective section 3:31-36 as a starting point for his discussion. This pericope, he suggests, is one in which at least five major motifs can be isolated: (1) Jesus comes (from above) and speaks (of the Father); (2) the Son makes the Father known; (3) the Father sent the Son; (4) the Father has given all things into the Son's hands; and (5) the Father and the Son.[35] Whatever one's final reaction to this selection of a basic pericope, the motifs listed do occur with frequency.

Loader's selection aids one in isolating motifs within the evangelist's Christology. It further aids one in locating that which is central in mission. In a discussion of witness and mission, one of the five is of special significance, that having to do with the "sending." This "sentness" has an agency aspect to it; it reflects the intimate relationship between the sender and the witness.

The "sentness" has the aspect of agency, as Peder Borgen has stressed.[36] His study underscores observations made also by others.[37] According to Borgen, the basic ingredient of this Jewish institution of agency is that "an agent is like the one who sent him." Consequently, to deal with the agent is the same as dealing with the sender himself. A second characteristic of agency centers around the specific mission of the agent. "It was the legal presumption that an agent should carry out his mission in obedience to his sender" (cf. 6:38; 8:29). A further element appears in the context of a lawsuit. According to this principle, the sender transferred his or her own rights, and the property involved, to the agent. On this basis, the agent might acquire the title in court and secure the claim for the self (see John 6:39). Yet for all the attention given to ownership and claims, the agent remains an agent (see 6:44). Thus, finally, the agent sent on a mission is to return to the sender.

It is apparent from these observations that the idea of agency is basic in understanding the context for Christological statements. It is basic also for understanding the different types of "sending" which appear. According to McPolin, there are actually four types of sending in this Gospel: "The Baptist is sent by God the Father to reveal Jesus as the Messiah; the Father sends the Son to reveal, to serve, to give life; the Holy Spirit is sent from the Father and the Son to communicate this life, to deepen and strengthen faith in Jesus; the disciples are sent to lead men to this new life, to transmit the revelation of Jesus."[38]

Since the sending of the Son is the leitmotif of this Gospel, the relationship between the Father and the Son remains a central concept. In this sense, the Father remains the sending center, the source from which all mission derives. But all other sendings revolve around Jesus, the Christ.

Because the sendings revolve around Jesus, the Christ, this motif illuminates the essential ingredients in the witness of those sent. It directs attention and incorporates the message about the one sent to be lifted up, so that the world not perish (the *what* of witness). It focuses on the realities and the privileges of a new relationship with Christ (the *how* of witness). That new relationship is one in which the "sent" Spirit is present. That Spirit assists disciples and interiorizes the work of Christ in them. This "sent" Spirit gives life-giving power which liberates from the power of sin and gives witness on behalf of the Christ. The motif of "sending" enables the evangelist to clarify the reality and responsibility of "being sent" in the world. Disciples represent the sender and go forth in *his authority.* They confront the world with the truth of Christ, so that decisions regarding the ultimate, the authentic, can and must be made in this earthly life.

Most of the descriptions of "sending" revolve around Jesus, the Christ. Because they do, it can be said finally that they provide the key toward understanding the complex nature of witness in the Fourth

Gospel. On the one hand, there is an offer of salvation to humankind. The offer is to include all. On the other, salvation consists only in separation from and in contrast to the ways of the world. Salvation is *for all* and yet *in separation from.* The latter is a linear thrust in the spiral movement of the Fourth Gospel. That is why the title and the subtitle of this chapter can be combined; Christ and mission and the Fourth Gospel, and our witness. That is why two significant passages, so prominent in any "mission" discussion, can be juxtaposed:

> I have given them thy word; and the world has hated them because they are not of the world, even as I am not of the world. . . .They are not of the world, even as I am not of the world. . .As thou didst send me into the world, so I have sent them into the world.
>
> (17:14-18)

> Peace be with you. As the Father has sent me, even so I send you.
>
> (20:21)

The Gospel of John may be said to offer an indirect mission theology. But this indirect thrust stands on the threshold of a commission that becomes direct in witness. The commission thus stands for all time: "As the Father has sent me, even so I send you."

5

MAKING DISCIPLES: THE MISSION OF THE CHURCH IN THE GOSPEL ACCORDING TO MATTHEW

Donald H. Juel

> All authority in heaven and on earth has been given to me. Go therefore and make disciples of all nations, baptizing them in the name of the Father and of the Son and of the Holy Spirit, teaching them to observe all that I have commanded you; and lo, I am with you always, to the close of the age.
>
> (Matt. 28:18-20)

Few words in the Bible are more familiar than Jesus' concluding instructions to his followers as recorded in Matthew 28. The Great Commission, as these verses are known, provides a natural focus for a discussion of the church and its mission. Before scrutinizing the verses to determine what they have to say to us, however, there are a few observations that should be made.

For one thing, the verses are part of a larger work—the "Gospel according to Matthew," as we call it. It is easy to deal with the Bible in bits and pieces, assuming that there is a nugget of truth to be extracted from every sentence. However, the Bible is made up of larger units—letters, stories, histories—in which smaller pieces are located. The last verses in Matthew's Gospel serve as the ending of a story; they sum up and conclude what has been narrated in the preceding 27 chapters. We do justice to the verses only within the context of the Gospel as a whole.

For another thing, we should be aware how much our terminology influences what we see and understand. We speak of Matthew's composition, for example, as a "gospel," and Matthew as one of the "evangelists." The New Testament does not use the words as we do. Gospel—"good news"—was used to refer to the message of salvation preached by Christians, not to a book. "Evangelist," from the Greek word meaning "messenger of good news," would suggest first of all a preacher who tells others about the message of salvation. We use the term in that way, referring to such people as Billy Graham as "evangelists," to distinguish them from others who may preach but whose primary audience is not unbelievers but groups of the faithful. "Evangelists" like Billy Graham feel called to make converts, then to leave the shepherding of the new flock to others. It would probably be more accurate to view Matthew as a pastor (shepherd) rather than as an evangelist. These concluding verses make little sense as directed to an audience of unbelievers; they make good sense as intended for the church. Like the other New Testament authors, Matthew wrote for the church; his purpose was not first to convert, but to help those who had believed and been baptized to understand what it meant to be a follower of the Christ. The story he tells is about how we got to where we are—and what we can now expect from life and what should be expected of us.

Go and Make Disciples

"Go therefore," Jesus says, offering last-minute instructions to his followers, who are gathered on a mountain to celebrate his return to the land of the living and to bid him farewell. "Go therefore," he says, speaking as one to whom all authority has been given. The "therefore" is important. It ties the command to everything that has gone before—Jesus' ministry of preaching and healing, his death accomplished as a ransom for many, his resurrection, and his statement that he has been given all authority in heaven and on earth. The command to go out presumes the good news about Jesus and the authority with which he gives commands and makes promises. The picture he sketches of the life of faith begins with a "therefore."

When Jesus sends his followers out in Matthew 10, he gives detailed instructions. He tells them where they are to go (only to the "lost sheep of the house of Israel" [Matt. 10:6]), what they are to do ("heal the sick, raise the dead, cleanse lepers, cast out demons," while preaching that "the kingdom of heaven is at hand" [Matt. 10:7-8]), what they are to bring with them ("take no gold, no bag for your journey, nor two tunics," etc. [10:9-10]), and how they are to support themselves (10:11-14). His instructions in 28:19-20 are not as detailed. What details there are, however, are important. Notice, for example, that Jesus tells his followers that they are to "make disciples." This is something rather different from the missionary task as outlined in chap. 10. The term *disciple* implies a relationship with a teacher. Jesus' "disciples" are told to go out to make their own. The "good news" is not pictured here as a message that can be declared to someone on a one-time basis. It requires teaching and learning; it includes a relationship. When we speak of "evangelism," it is important to have in mind images of what the enterprise involves. According to Matt. 28:19, it involves establishing new circles of people who will learn about the faith and will grow.

The image of discipleship—a process of learning that presumes a relationship between learner and teacher—provides a crucial insight into the meaning of Baptism, another aspect of the mission Jesus sketches for his followers here at the end of Matthew's Gospel. What does it mean to "baptize in the name of the Father and of the Son and of the Holy Spirit"? What pictures come to mind? Practice is usually a far more powerful teacher than theory. How we understand Baptism probably has more to do with what happens in congregations than with what the New Testament or the catechism may say. Consider the familiar scene: a strange couple shows up in church one Sunday morning with an infant to be baptized. Most members of the congregation have never seen the people before. They come forward with sponsors from out of town, a little ceremony takes place, and no one ever sees parents, sponsors, or child again. The promises made by parents, sponsors, and congregation to bring the child up within the faith may or may not be kept. The matter is apparently not important enough to the congregation for it to follow up.

Such rites are to embody our theology, but practices like the one described above do not reflect the way our heritage or the New Testament speak of Baptism. Baptism is entrance into the body of Christ; a relationship is established both with Jesus and with his church. At Baptism, God establishes a bond with us that lasts for ever—a bond that promises life. And that relationship is embodied in membership in the body of Christ. Our special relationship to God through Baptism takes the form of membership in specific congregations where the gospel is preached, the sacraments celebrated, and where Christians gather for mutual care and growth. The mission of the church is to establish relationships—not simply between individuals and God, but among individuals whom God has called into a family. Simply telling people about Jesus is hardly what Jesus has in mind here in our text. While our particular form of congregational life may not be the only alternative available, establishing congregations as our way of doing evangelism is not far off the mark. Jesus does not provide a complete definition of Baptism in Matthew; we must learn about that from the rest of the New Testament. But the command to baptize and to make disciples presumes that the two are related; the two are aspects of the same enterprise.

Some Christian traditions speak of evangelism and the mission of the church almost exclusively in terms of conversion. Simply becoming a Christian does not settle things, however. Paul wrote fierce letters to Christians who he believed had been led astray and were in danger of deserting the faith; he wrote to others who found in their status as forgiven sinners new ways to exalt themselves over others. Baptism is an introduction to discipleship, and there is much to be learned about living as a child of God. The New Testament Gospels and Epistles were written by believers convinced that faith in Jesus made a difference in the way life was to be lived. Luther wrote a catechism to be used by heads of families to teach children about living as Christians. Matthew was no less interested in the shape of discipleship. Jesus' followers were instructed to "teach all that I have commanded you." In Jesus' teachings, Matthew believed Christians could find some guidelines for the life of faith. Offering such guidelines was perhaps one of the most important reasons for writing his "Gospel."

The Teacher

The first event in Jesus' public ministry as Mark describes it is an exorcism in a synagogue. In Mark, Jesus is engaged in warfare with Satan and his hosts. He is portrayed as a traveling miracle worker and healer. It is different with Matthew. Jesus heals and casts out demons, but he is preeminently a teacher. The first act of his ministry that Matthew chooses to report in detail is a lengthy sermon, known as the Sermon on the Mount, which speaks about discipleship. The instructions are both specific and challenging. Four more times in Matthew a block of material is sectioned off from the narrative for special emphasis (10; 13; 18; 24–25). Each of the sections has something to do with discipleship. There are instructions to the disciples regarding their mission of preaching and healing (10), parables about the kingdom of heaven (13), instructions about the internal life of the church (18), and instructions about what the future holds for Jesus' followers (24–25). The formalized conclusions to each of these sections ("when Jesus had finished all these sayings," etc.) highlight their significance in the structure of the book. Matthew's Jesus is a teacher; he gives instructions regarding the life to which his followers are invited.

The historical situation in which Matthew was written may help to explain some features of his work. The Gospel was probably composed sometime between 80 and 90 C.E. during a period of considerable uncertainty within the Jewish and Christian communities. The temple in Jerusalem had been destroyed (70 C.E.). For all those who traced their identity to Abraham, the fateful war against Rome, concluded with the suicide of the defenders of the fortress at Masada (73 C.E.), marked a decisive turning point. No longer would sacrifices be offered for sin. Identity as the people of God would come to be marked by a way of life and a holy book. Soon after the temple's destruction, a small group of Jewish sages began serving as Israel's religious court in a small town on the Mediterranean coast known as Jabneh (Jamnia). They began a process of redefining what it meant to be a Jew, a process that would result in what later generations would refer to as "orthodox Judaism." Their task centered on ethics—laying out in detail how a Jew was to live.

Matthew's enterprise may be some form of response to these events, recognizing the need to make sense of a chaotic world in terms of some structures for living but also acknowledging the growing distance between "their synagogues" and "our" gatherings. Matthew's Gospel was written at a time when the break between Jews who believed in Jesus and those who did not was becoming inevitable. What had begun as a Jewish messianic sect would later come to be known as "Christian" and would in a few more decades become a non-Jewish religious movement. Matthew stands at the transition, writing for people who needed some sense of who they were and what mission God had in mind for them.

Since his Gospel was first written, it has been the favorite of the church. The reason is perhaps its utility. Matthew spoke not only to his own generation but to the later church as well. We will examine some aspects of his Gospel that seem particularly relevant today to those interested in what it means to live as God's people.

A Forgiving Community

Jesus told stories that people remembered. One was about a shepherd whose behavior made little sense measured by conventional standards (Matt. 18:10-14). When the shepherd discovers that one of his hundred sheep is lost, he leaves the rest of the flock and goes in search of the one. The story says nothing about taking care to protect the rest of the flock in his absence. He leaves them on the hillside and goes after the one. He seems to care more for the one than for the ninety-nine: "And if he finds it, truly I say to you, he rejoices over it more than over the ninety-nine that never went astray." The single-mindedness of the shepherd seems almost foolish, but that is the way it is with God, says the parable. God is preoccupied with the lost, a preoccupation reflected in Jesus' ministry.

In Luke, Jesus tells the parable in response to the grumbling of religious people about his association with the unwashed (sinners and tax collectors; Luke 15:3-7). In Matthew, the same story is told to illustrate how important one of the "little ones," a term used for Christians, should be to those within the Christian family. The issue in Matthew is not outreach as much as care for strays within the family. The parable is followed by detailed instructions for settling disputes within the family—what to do when "one of your brothers sins against you."

The scope of the church's mission is vast: we are called to bring the gospel to the ends of the earth, making disciples of all the nations. The church's mission is also close at hand. It involves establishing lasting bonds among the faithful in a society where stability is a rare commodity. At the same time the church stresses the need to reach beyond the confines of the economic and racial boundaries of American Lutheranism, it cannot forget the sustained ministry to those within the family. Even in small towns where almost every name appears on a church roster, where evangelism promises limited success, there are people whose names have been placed on inactive lists because they have chosen not to participate in the life of the church—often because of an exchange of harsh words or a misunderstanding or because no effort has been made to make them feel at home. Most of these people have been baptized into the body of Christ, stamped with the sign of the cross forever, bonded to others in the family for all time.

Such strays, Jesus tells his followers, are of utmost concern to God. Every measure should be taken to bring them back. The realities of evil are not minimized. There are serious hurts we inflict on one another that cannot be ignored; they must be healed. That can occur only when the hurt is acknowledged, when forgiveness is requested and accepted. The procedures outlined for dealing with such conflicts in Matt. 18:15-18 may seem surprisingly detailed. The point, however, is that we need some structures for dealing with one another. Church polity as spelled out in constitutions for individual congregations and for larger organizational units of the church is a gift by which the weak can be protected against the strong and by which we can regularly be confronted with our tendency to dominate or to back out of relationships rather than risk confrontation. Christians enter a new family at Baptism; God has bound us to our new brothers and sisters. And the new community in Christ is called to be characterized by forgiveness. Forgiveness is not a reflex; it is something that must be learned and practiced.

The number of passages in Matthew which deal with forgiveness is striking. Jesus speaks about hostility among brothers in terms of the commandment not to kill (5:21-26): hatred can do as much damage as outright murder. The prayer Jesus teaches his disciples speaks about God's forgiveness of us and about our forgiveness of others (6:9-15). Jesus' instructions about common life (chap. 18) include a parable about a servant whose staggering debt to his master was canceled but who demands payment of a small debt from a fellow slave who owes him money. The parable offers dire warnings about what the end of such behavior shall be (18:22-25).

The emphasis is typical of Matthew. The point is not that Christians should strive for moral perfection because that is the only way true community can be achieved. The existence of the family is possible only because Jesus has come to "give his life as a ransom for many" (Matt. 20:28). The last meal he shares with his disciples commemorates his offering of himself "for the remission of sins" (26:28). The teacher is first of all the one who gives himself to deliver us from sin and death. But there are then implications for the community that names itself after the crucified and risen Christ. Believers are to be conformed to Christ, to use Pauline language. The church is to be a place where forgiveness occurs—where we are forgiven and thus can learn to forgive others. Forgiveness does not come naturally, which is why it requires discipline—and even structure.

The picture Matthew sketches of the church in chap. 18 is probably different from our own conception of the congregation of which we are members. Jesus establishes an aggressive community that is more concerned with strays and those engaged in hurtful conflicts than with the stable membership. God's preoccupation is seeking and saving the lost—healing wounds, putting out fires, bringing about reconciliation. The church described here is not afraid to speak words of judgment when they are required. Discipline is not measured by the canons of politeness and civility but in terms of its effectiveness: it may be that telling the truth and aggressive seeking and saving of the lost will result in the salvation of some who would have remained outside. The health of the family depends upon its ability to bandage up hurts and reestablish ties.

Outreach is basic to the life of the church. Even where there are few new faces in the community, however, there are always many strays who need to be brought back into the fold where they can be nurtured and cared for.

Living in Anticipation

The last of Jesus' discourses in Matthew is recorded in chaps. 24–25, just prior to the fateful events that were to lead to his arrest, trial, and death. The words addressed to his disciples about what was to happen in the future are clearly intended for the later church. As in Mark, the coming days are painted in somber colors: Jesus promises that those days will bring the destruction of the temple and great trials. His words focus on trials of the faithful. Believers must be prepared for temptation: false Christs and false prophets will arise (24:4-5,9-11,23-25). Jesus' followers will be persecuted and killed and "hated by all the nations because of my name" (24:9-10). The future also holds promise for those who endure: at the end, the Son of man will send his angels to gather the elect from every corner of the earth (24:29-31).

Though the tone of Jesus' warnings is hardly upbeat, the picture is not the one sketched in John's Apocalypse. The days ahead are not so totally without prospect. There is no prophecy that God will give to the "beast" (symbolizing the powers of this age) the ability to make war on the saints and prevail over them (Rev. 13:7). The future is seen as a time of opportunity, and the great temptation is to become complacent or weary. "Stay awake," Jesus admonishes his followers, "for you do not know at what hour your Lord is coming" (24:42).

All the parables that follow emphasize responsibility. The kingdom of heaven is like 10 virgins whose job is to light the wedding procession when the bridegroom emerges. Their responsibility is to be ready when the time comes (25:1-13). Or it is like a master who gives his servants charge of his property and returns to demand an accounting of their stewardship (25:14-30). The followers to whom such parables are addressed are anything but helpless. There are tasks to perform, and Jesus promises the authority and the resources necessary to do the tasks to which disciples are called. Christians have often thought about themselves largely as victims and have understood words about the future in terms of comfort and consolation. The tone in Jesus' illustrations is rather challenging. He does not encourage sheer bravado in the face of evil: there is recognition that events will often be beyond the control of the faithful. Confidence is appropriate only because Jesus promises that he will return at the end to gather his elect from the corners of the earth (24:29-31). But because there is reason for confidence, the faithful are admonished to prepare for responsible stewardship of what has been entrusted to them.

The first two parables in chap. 25 speak of responsibility in general terms. Jesus' account of the judgment scene that ends his discourse is more specific. Discipleship is not simply preaching the gospel and making disciples. It is caring for those about whom Christ cared. In the familiar story of the last judgment, those commended for doing God's will are surprised by what they are told:

> For I was hungry, and you gave me food, I was thirsty and you gave me drink, I was a stranger and you welcomed me, I was naked and you clothed me, I was sick and you visited me, I was in prison and you came to me.
>
> (Matt. 25:34-36)

The surprise, for both the righteous and the unrighteous, is that concern for Christ is demonstrated in ordinary concern for the neighbor. "God does not need our good works," Luther insisted, "but our neighbor does."

The life to which the church is called is in every respect ordinary. The place the life of faith is lived out is the world we inhabit, the world in which we function as members of families, as friends, as employers and employees, as citizens of a community, a nation, and a world. Such ordinary tasks as showing hospitality to newcomers or to those who have few friends are commended to us as the will of God. The God we worship is not enthroned in some distant place, watching our struggles with benign indifference. God is engaged in the struggles, concerned about the hungry and the naked and the prisoners and the lonely.

There are possibilities of service at every level. The church is called to encourage the most creative and imaginative in our society to devise ways to share our wealth with the poor in other countries without destroying their local economies or bankrupting ours. Political solutions to problems of poverty and injustice and international tensions will do more than the sum total of all charities. The church must encourage the brightest and the most responsible people to work for the neighbor at such levels. At the same time, the community of believers is called to provide a family for those who have none, to welcome in the stranger and the broken, to demonstrate ordinary hospitality for those near at hand—all in the name of the one who died for us, who lives among us, and who will one day finish what he began. "Truly, I say to you, as you did it to one of the least of these my brethren, you did it to me" (Matt. 25:40).

"To the Close of the Age"

The verses we call the Great Commission serve as the conclusion of a book. If you think about it, the conclusion does not provide a completely satisfying ending. Matthew's version of the story may be somewhat less uncomfortable than Mark's, which originally ended with frightened women who say nothing to anyone (Mark 16:8). Yet the last verse in Matthew offers no sense of finality; loose ends are left untied. Matthew does not finish the story, following Jesus back to his place in the heavenly court. We are left with Jesus on a mountain, among his disciples, giving commands and making promises.

We would be more comfortable, perhaps, with a genuine ending. Unfinished stories are too much like real life, where broken commitments, disappointed expectations, and regrets are the norm. We write stories, argued one critic, to convince ourselves that things have satisfying endings and that the world makes sense. Deep down we suspect it is not so, which is why our stories can seem so precious.

Matthew's Gospel does not offer the kind of peace for which we might long—a peace that comes either from the final death of hope or the final triumph of the truth. It leaves us where we are, stuck between the promise and its fulfillment. But it offers such hope as there is to give. It provides testimony that Jesus could not be bound by death, and it ends with a promise: "Truly I am with you to the close of the age." The story ends in anticipation, but not the sort that requires sheer defiance of all we know and experience. Jesus is here. We learn early in the story that Jesus will be called Emmanuel, a name that means "God with us" (Matt. 1:23). Jesus likewise promises his disciples that "where two or three are gathered in my name, there am I in the midst of them" (Matt. 18:20). That presence is known in many ways: through the reading of the scriptural testimony preserved for us in the Bible, in the sacraments, in the preached word, perhaps even in the existence of the body of Christ, the church. We are not left to imagine where God can be known and encountered; faith is not sheer anticipation of what is yet to be. Faith is born and nourished within the womb of the gathered community of the faithful, where God is present in word and sacrament.

We need constantly to be reminded that the object of Christian faith is the God who created the heavens and the earth and in whose hands the future lies. God's work is not restricted to the church but encompasses all the nations. The church is commanded to share that concern for all the world and not to become imprisoned within the narrow confines of one structure. God has far-reaching plans, and God's will will be done only when the Son of man sends his angels to gather the elect from the four winds. Until then, life is lived in anticipation, between the times. Yet in that intervening time, which is our time, the focus of God's work is the concrete setting in which life is lived and the relationships by which life is sustained. Perhaps that is why the church in its specific congregational manifestations is the focus of Matthew's interest. And perhaps that is why his Gospel has always been the church's favorite.

6

BIBLICAL MOTIFS IN MODERN MISSION THEOLOGY

Gordon S. Huffman Jr.

"Even a few decades ago, the North Atlantic churches were the arbiters of Christian theology. Today the situation is totally different."[1] With the transition from "sending" and "receiving" churches to a global Christian community mutually engaged in mission has come a shift in the use of the Bible for mission understanding and engagement. There has emerged in recent years a richly patterned appropriation of biblical materials and motifs for mission theology. Many of these motifs emerge from situations of ferment and conflict, especially in the Third World, rather than from offices and studies in Europe and North America. As Emilo Castro puts it:

> Behind each of these theologies—liberation, African, Black, feminist, minjung—there is a situation of conflict. No new theological system has emerged in the last twenty years that does not condemn some kind of oppression and affirm some specific perspective of the gospel which emerges out of the problems faced by the groups doing the theological work.[2]

Moreover, these new theological perspectives "are basically missiologies. They are not explanations of God's being, but represent a passionate search for new options for the mission of the churches."[3] Thus modern mission theology, anticipating what is beginning to happen in other theological disciplines, finds itself in the fascinating position of engaging in a genuine global dialog among equals. The result is that many of the focal points and motifs of modern mission theology are those brought to our attention by brothers and sisters from the Third World.

Hermeneutical Considerations

Before considering particular examples of the biblical motifs most prominent in global mission theology today, it is necessary to look at the way in which the hermeneutical process itself has been altered by the development of recent theological work in the Third World.

With the rise and acceptance of the historical-scientific approach to the understanding of Scripture, a process covering much of the last century, the claim of First World/North Atlantic schools to be the arbiters of the interpretation of Scripture was strengthened. Moving from an earlier claim to possess superior knowledge on the basis of cultural superiority and historical precedence, First World academics now could assert on scientific grounds that they understood Scripture better because of a scholarly understanding which penetrated beneath the surface meaning and words of the text to its underlying intent and meaning. Associated with this process and claim, although not usually articulated in these words, was a growing belief that the knowledge gained through the exercise of the full scholarly arsenal was an "objective" understanding of the Scriptures, capable (to a great degree) of being universalized and of being understood and accepted without regard to one's cultural matrix. The corollary, strongly felt although not expressed overtly, was that the interpretation of Scripture attained by scholars in Europe and North America was essentially free from cultural, economic, or political bias, and was in that sense also "objective." By extension, the intuitive readings and understandings of persons less well trained and qualified might be interesting—and might afford some insight into the cultural perspectives of persons from other cultures and other subcultural situations—but such interpretations were ultimately subject to correction by the true scholars of the Scriptures.

Such a perspective meant that for quite some time the arbiters of scriptural hermeneutics (as, indeed, the developers of virtually every facet of theological work) were white, middle- or upper-middle-class males of European stock. It did not occur to such persons that the sociological accidents of their origin and life situation might in themselves serve as a filtering mechanism for the way in which they heard and read, understood and articulated the message of the Scripture and of the gospel itself.

Today that view and attitude is challenged even by First World scholars, and especially as a result of questions raised by Third World scholars and theologians. The "myth of objectivity" is under attack, and with it the hitherto unassailable right of First World scholars to function as sole arbiters of theological truth and biblical understandings. The challenge has developed as Third World persons have become fully qualified in the guild system of Western theology, but have still raised objections to that theology both with respect to its method and its content. Among the more important questions put to Western theology by the newly assertive theologians of the Third World are these:

- Why have you not noticed the prominence of certain biblical themes like its strong economic concern, the significance of the poor (not excluding Jesus and the early church), and the centrality of liberation as an action of God?
- What is the relationship between the Scriptures, especially the Old Testament, and the history of those peoples (like the Chinese) who have a separate history and heritage? Are such peoples' histories outside the ambit of God's concern prior to the arrival of North Atlantic missionaries? Has God been absent from their histories for thousands of years?
- How is it that the concern of the Western churches for orthodoxy has not issued in an equivalent concern for orthopraxis? Is it not possible that a theology which claims to represent a unity of action and reflection and practice is *by definition* inadequate? What is the meaning of the western dichotomy between intellectual formulation and the Christian life?

Such questions are merely illustrative of the challenges put to Western theology from the Third World perspective. These have been accompanied by the recognition of Third World scholars that their own milieus had more in common with biblical times and settings than did Western industrial and postindustrial society, and that frequently their languages, thought patterns, value systems, and networks of relationships more closely resembled those found in the Bible than did those of the North Atlantic community.

At the same time that such realizations were developing in the Third World, there has been a growing understanding in the West of the limitations of a hermeneutical perspective that reflects only a single sociological situation. The sociology of knowledge asserts that even within a single culture an individual's location in that society conditions that person's outlook. Thus there are elements from a position of dominance or oppression that reflect the perspectives and concerns of those groups; such elements tend to shape, even to distort, the worldview of these groups. It is then a clearly subjective rather than a "real" or "objective" view of the world. This constitutes a mechanism that filters out threatening or uncongenial elements of reality, one that suggests more congenial alternate interpretations. That means that we, unconsciously and even unwillingly, interpret everything, *including the Bible,* through the lenses of our cultural and class perspectives.[4]

One of the important remedies for such a limitation to our interpretive abilities is an interclass and cross-cultural reading of the Bible which provides the mutual correctives of discovering and pointing out one another's blind spots and misreadings.[5]

Beyond the problems inherent in any attempt to do hermeneutical work from any single perspective is a deeper and more disturbing question: Does not relative affluence pose a particular problem for hearing and understanding, let alone appropriating, the good news first announced to the poor? In the words of Charles R. Taber, "there seems to be a real sense in which complacent enjoyment of any sort of unfair advantage over others—economic, social, political, or intellectual—may in itself constitute an impediment to the understanding of the good news."[6] Most Western theologians, viewed from a global perspective, enjoy all of those advantages.

By contrast, the poor, though not inherently wiser or more virtuous, lack the impediment of worldly goods and need fewer illusions to justify their anomalous position in society. Having fewer vested interests in the status quo, they may be in a "better position not only to receive the gospel but even to understand it."[7] In other words, the social and cultural position of Western scholars may make us less able than persons in the Third World to hear and understand the gospel.

That does not imply that Western scholars should abandon the tools of biblical scholarship and interpretation, but that we must learn to listen with genuine respect—and even expectation—when sisters and brothers from other social realities and cultures tell us what they hear in the Bible. "We have grown so accustomed to being the world's experts, the world's teachers, that it may be a salutary exercise for us to sit at the feet of the world's destitute, the world's oppressed, the world's babes, and so learn of Christ."[8] That is what global mission theology has been doing in recent years, and what the broader theological disciplines are beginning to do.[9] (While Third World theologians do not as a rule qualify as destitute, oppressed, or babes, their more intimate contact with such realities has enabled a constructive global dialog to develop in which new sociological and cultural perspectives enrich the international effort to understand and appropriate the biblical message.) The biblical motifs to which we now turn have emerged as prominent in modern mission theology through a genuinely global process of study, sharing, and learning.

Overarching Themes

In reviewing the development of mission theology in recent years, I want to identify four overarching themes that persist through a variety of biblical motifs. Each theme has its own identity, but each is also related to the others. All of the themes are relevant to each of the biblical motifs that will be examined next. While none of the themes is especially startling in itself, taken together they represent something of a missiological consensus and perspective that shapes the interpretation of specific biblical passages.

God Is Active in History

The first of the overarching themes is that *God is active in history.* This assertion takes seriously the biblical accounts of God's activity in the history of Israel and the surrounding nations, and takes with equal seriousness the promises for God's continued and ongoing activity. The history envisioned is the human and temporal existence in which we all participate. Without arguing whether God can or cannot operate outside history, this thematic understanding asserts that God has chosen to operate in and through human history as we know it. This activity of God is not episodic and apparently whimsical—as if God lived elsewhere and occasionally dropped down to intervene in our history—

but is part of the warp and woof of the lives of persons, societies, and nations, as it was seen to be by the biblical writers. Gustavo Gutierrez uses the slogan "History is one"[10] to indicate the transcending of a view which saw God's history and human history running on separate tracks with only an occasional intersection.

God Is Active through Human Agents

A second overarching theme, something of a corollary of the first, but going beyond it, is that *God is active through human agents.* To assert that God is active in history can remain abstract until one asks how God's will is accomplished in the world. Again, setting aside the theoretical question of God's ability to act through alternative modalities, one is compelled by the biblical witnesses to draw the conclusion that God frequently chooses to act through the medium of human beings, consciously or unconsciously called and made useful to serve God's purpose in the world. Those who commit themselves consciously to try to discern and to accomplish that purpose ("Thy will be done, on earth as it is in heaven") or in Paul's words to serve as the body of Christ, as the hands and feet of Jesus in his physical absence, constitute the Christian community. They recognize, of course, the imperfect way in which they are useful for God's activity, and acknowledge, sometimes even with gratitude, God's choice of other human agents. Whether it is through the Christian community or outside it, however, the clear fact is that God is active in the world through human agents. The recognition of that fact affects both the way in which Christians attempt to follow their calling and to shaping their lives, and the value given to any and all human activity.

Hope

A third overarching theme running through all the major biblical motifs of modern mission theology is the theme of hope, which has been so well articulated by Jürgen Moltmann. Here is not a focus on posthistorical events framed in mythological categories, but a focus on the shaping of the present and the near-term future—the guiding of the development of history—informed by the eschatological vision of the way things will be when God's rule is fully realized. This is accompanied and even propelled by a confidence that God's will shall be the final outcome of history, and that those who conform their will to God's will need have no ultimate anxiety, despite the difficulties of the present. The present, despite appearances to the contrary, can be shaped by the knowledge of what the future holds. The eschatological community is a community from the future which lives in the present. It can live in the quiet confidence of those who know the outcome of the still-unfolding story. Thus it continues to work in the present toward that outcome, even when everything seems to be going the other direction. It knows it is on the side of history.

Universal and Missionary Gospel

The fourth overarching theme is that of the universal and missionary character of the Christian message. Accompanying the movement beyond cultural blindness has come a renewed appreciation of the fact that the biblical vision is a comprehensive one. It begins with the creation stories, moves through the Table of Nations (Genesis 10) and the call of Abraham, continues through the prophetic reformations and into the New Testament. There the strictly Jewish perspective is broadened to a global and even cosmic vision of the extent of the gospel's power, and all peoples are seen as the goal of God's saving work. While that has always been acknowledged in missionary circles, the universal extent of the saving work of God has come to have new meaning in the era in which mature churches and competent leaders and theologians are to be found on all continents and among most peoples. A consequent issue is the relationship of the universal to the particular. What, for example, does God's saving action, expressed in the particular form of Israel's history, say to African cultures? Does God's universally intended salvation take the same shape for every time and place, or can there be particular variations?

Closely tied to the understanding that the divine intention for all persons is that they know God's love, is the sense of the missionary nature of the church. Motivated to be active for God in history, the church is to see itself as sent out into the world to follow God's mission. The missionary vocation is not to be understood as unusual; it is part of the Christian vocation to be sent by God. Thus the church, locally and globally, is impelled beyond itself for the sake of the world. It reaches out with the message of God's good work and seeks to shape history in accordance with God's will.

Biblical Motifs

Any attempt to select those biblical motifs that have had the greatest significance in modern mission theology is bound to be subjective. Nevertheless, it would seem that seven motifs stand out as having had the greatest impact on mission theology in recent years. While they have some interrelationships among themselves, they are woven together both by the altered hermeneutical process referred to above and especially by the four overarching themes just discussed.

Exodus and Liberation

The first, and in some ways the most obvious, of the biblical motifs is the Exodus motif, which is generally understood to be a liberation motif. The last generation of Old Testament scholarship discovered the Exodus to be the central and formative event of the Old Testament. God's deliverance of the people who would become Israel was an act which both claimed and formed that people and, at the same time, served as a paradigm of the way God worked and works in the world. God was revealed in the Exodus to be a saving God, a God active in the world and in history, a God of concern and love. The Exodus would be called to remembrance by the people of Israel not merely for national celebration but especially to keep alive the revelation of the nature of the Lord of all creation: God is a God of deliverance.

Oppressed peoples throughout the ages around the world have found in the Exodus story an event and a possibility to which they were irresistibly drawn. The Exodus was at the center of preaching in the church of the black slaves in North America. It has been fundamental in the faith experience of people living under oppressive conditions in Latin America and colonial Africa, as well as Asia. Oppressed people find ready identification with the lot of the Hebrew people in Egypt, they thrill to the story of liberation under the reluctant leadership of Moses, and they are deeply moved and even transformed by the understanding that the same God is active in history today and may act in a similar way to deliver them from bondage. For them the Exodus story is not mere ancient history with a theological message; rather it tells of God's saving work (cf. Exod. 14:13,30) for people like themselves, and creates and sustains hope for them in the present. God sees and hears.[11] At the same time, the proclamation of the Exodus motif has been considered dangerous and even subversive in some circumstances both in the North American context of slavery and in the Central America of today.[12]

It is especially as mission theology has moved from being an exercise conducted in Europe and North America to being the product of a global dialog that the significance of the Exodus story as a critical motif for missiology has emerged. Particularly prominent in emphasizing its themes have been theologians in Latin America and in southern Africa. Gustavo Gutierrez sees in the Exodus a link between creation and salvation.[13] He finds in the liberation from Egypt both a historical fact and a fertile biblical theme, and he cultivates that theme from the perspective of Latin American people needing historical and theological liberation.[14] Like Gutierrez, Desmond Tutu finds in both the activity of God and the reactions of the Hebrew people in the Exodus story a paradigm for the present and future of his own people.[15]

The reemergence of the Exodus motif has brought with it a rediscovery of the language of liberation. As Orlando Costas puts it in his fine volume *The Integrity of Mission,*

> The concept of liberation is not new to the Bible. In a sense, it can be found in it from beginning to end since the Bible is concerned with the history of God's liberating deeds. Up to recently, however, the word *liberation* has remained largely dormant or at least hidden behind other words such as salvation, redemption, reconciliation and regeneration.[16]

Together with the rediscovery that much of the biblical witness attains new clarity and power when understood in terms of liberation has come a renewed study of the meaning of the motif of salvation in the Bible. For a very long time this excellent biblical image labored under the burden of privatistic and spiritualistic interpretation, as though the entire biblical message could be reduced to an individual soul's being cleansed and saved from eternal perdition. As the Bible came to be read and interpreted more by persons in the Third World, however, the perspective of these people, less privileged and even oppressed, illuminated in new ways the meaning of many portions of Scripture and revealed aspects of the scriptural witness hitherto hidden from view. One of those aspects was the series of events that may be described as liberation, and the deep biblical concern for persons in need of God's liberating power. Recognizing the Exodus as merely the most obvious of many such acts of God, the theologians now known as liberationists proposed to the global church the motif of liberation as a helpful and central scriptural motif by which to understand and interpret God's ongoing historical activity. It is therefore also a significant element of the mission to which the church is called. It is not necessary to resolve the continuing debate over the details of liberation theology in order to see that the Exodus and liberation motif together constitute the most compelling element of current mission theology.

Salvation and Evangelization

Closely related to the Exodus/liberation motif is that of salvation and evangelization. The church in mission has always been concerned for the salvation of those who have not heard the gospel, and has endeavored to communicate that salvation in ways that can form the basis for personal transformation. In recent decades serious attention has been given to the study of the precise nature and content of that salvation and to the means for communicating the message of salvation.

"Salvation Today" was the theme of the Assembly of the Commission on World Mission and Evangelism (CWME) of the World Council of Churches when it met in Bangkok, Thailand, in 1973. A decade earlier the CWME meeting in Mexico City had asked the question, "What is the form and content of the salvation which Christ offers to men and women in the secular world?" For several years prior to Bangkok serious study went into the understanding of *salvation,* a term once considered so self-evident as to need little definition. Bangkok drew together more than 300 participants from 69 countries. For the first time at a CWME Assembly, a majority (52%) of the participants came from Asia, Africa, and Latin America. There was a rich diversity of experience and of approach to the theological task of understanding and explicating salvation. That richness was evident in the attempt to develop an expression of salvation that was comprehensive, which pulled together the individual and social, personal and corporate, churchly and secular aspects of salvation. Although conference documents usually satisfy no one entirely, the Bangkok statements attempted to give expression to the variety of views held by professing Christians on the nature of salvation. Participants attempted to hold together the two aspects of mission: evangelism and social action.

> Our concentration upon the social, economic and political implications of the gospel does not in any way deny the personal and eternal dimensions of salvation. Rather, we would emphasize that the personal, social, individual and corporate aspects of salvation are so interrelated that they are inseparable.[17]

In an attempt to express aspects of salvation previously overlooked in the developed countries of the north, the assembly gave strong voice to the social dimensions of salvation. Although that emphasis provoked much criticism, especially from conservative evangelical thinkers, it did succeed in dramatizing the breadth of meaning attaching to the biblical image of salvation, and led those in the conciliar stream of mission thought to a far more comprehensive view of salvation.

If salvation is understood to be comprehensive in scope, then evangelism or evangelization must become more than verbal proclamation aimed at eliciting verbal affirmation of the faith. As the World Council dealt with the issue in Uppsala in 1968, so did conservative evangelicals at the Lausanne Congress on World Evangelization in 1974 and the Roman Catholic Church in its Third General Conference of the Synod of Bishops, also held in 1974, meeting around the theme "The Evangelization of the Modern World."

At Lausanne almost half the participants and more than one-third of the plenary papers came from Asia, Africa, and Latin America, and the impact of the non-Western participants was clear. While affirming the traditional understandings of the evangelical movement, Lausanne also struggled with the demands of the total needs of the total human community. John R. W. Stott, who at the Berlin Congress in 1966 had argued that the Great Commission required exclusive attention to conversion through preaching and teaching, reversed himself at Lausanne:

> Today, however, I would express myself differently. . . . I now see more clearly that not only the consequences of the commission but the actual commission itself must be understood to include social as well as evangelistic responsibility, unless we are to be guilty of distorting the words of Jesus.[18]

According to Rodger C. Bassham, "this comprehensive understanding of mission [at Lausanne], flowing from the activity and purpose of God, provided a new orientation for evangelical mission theology."[19]

Meeting just weeks later, the Synod of Bishops wrestled with the same issues, and experienced genuine difficulty. It was unable to approve a final document, entrusting that to Pope Paul VI, in what became the Apostolic Exhortation *Evangelii Nuntiandi,* which summarized the synod's discussions. The Synod, however, did produce a declaration, which spoke of

> the mutual relationship between evangelization and integral salvation or the complete liberation of man and of peoples. In a matter of such importance we experienced profound unity in reaffirming the intimate connection between evangelization and such liberation.[20]

Thus the World Council, the evangelical movement, and the Roman Catholic Church, all at about the same time and through a sometimes painful process in which the influence of Third World theologians was significant to an unprecedented degree, agreed that the motif of salvation, always central, points to the comprehensive saving activity of God in the world. They further concluded that the church is called to give expression to the good news of that salvation in a comprehensive way, a way that speaks meaningfully to the full range of human conditions and needs in the world.

Justice and Righteousness

A third biblical motif which has emerged with great force in modern mission theology is that of justice and righteousness. In the first instance this refers to the character of God as a just and righteous God, and in the second, to the consequent awareness that persons and groups following God's mission in the world will find concerns for justice and right relationships integral to their mission. Justice and righteousness, of course, are themes which stand out in any attentive reading of the Bible. Particularly in the Old Testament—in the stories of God's dealing with people and peoples, in the Psalms and wisdom literature, and in the prophetic call for renewal of commitment—God's very nature is seen as intrinsically just. God's people, therefore, have no alternative but to seek justice and righteousness. One of the passages frequently cited as an illustration of this motif is Jer. 22:13-17, in which the prophet argues that "to know God," which means to love God, is to do justice and righteousness.[21]

As with the preceding motif, so also with that of justice and righteousness there has been a development of understanding sparked by the perspective of Third World theologians. It is evident in all three streams of mission theology: conciliar, evangelical, and Roman Catholic. In the conciliar movement the concern for justice came to the fore in the 60s, and was especially evident in the Uppsala Assembly of the World Council of Churches in 1968. Since that time there has been a moderation or balancing of language, but no retreat from the commitment that justice in all its aspects is a prominent part of the churches' agenda. This commitment has shown itself in various ways: in support for the liberation movements in southern Africa, in concern over Vietnam and Central America, in efforts to understand and ameliorate hunger and poverty, in a more critical appraisal of capitalism as it operates in Third World settings, and in a more vocal participation in debates about public policy and spending. Some have gone so far as to argue that to do justice is the new function of the church in North American Christianity.[22]

Evangelical mission theology has had a harder time understanding and incorporating the motifs of justice and righteousness. Yet the working out of the Lausanne conclusions, especially under the influence of such Latin American evangelicals as Rene Padilla and Samuel Escobar, has produced remarkable change among some evangelical thinkers. Waldron Scott, General Secretary of the World Evangelical Fellowship, argued in *Bring Forth Justice* that "the biblical understanding of mission is rectification, the establishment of justice."[23] He contends that justice and righteousness together form a hendiadys which is the equivalent of "social justice," and that "discipleship is not fully biblical apart from a commitment to social justice."[24] In the follow-up meetings organized by the Lausanne Committee for World Evangelism (Pattaya, Thailand, in June 1980, and Grand Rapids in June 1982) the further implications of the Christian concern for justice were considered. Grand Rapids affirmed that "evangelism and social responsibility, while distinct from one another, are integrally related in our proclamation of and obedience to the gospel. The partnership is in reality a marriage."[25] In Roman Catholic thought, concern for justice was articulated at Vatican II, but given fuller treatment only in later conferences. The Medellin (1968) and Puebla (1979) meetings of the Latin American bishops gave careful attention to the issues of injustice and justice in Latin

America. It was the 1971 Synod of Bishops of the whole church, however, meeting around the theme "Justice in the World," that committed the church to "action toward justice." In the words of Philip Scharper, founding editor of Orbis Press:

> The bishops said the transformation of the world is a constitutive element of the teaching of the Gospel, that the church's mission is to effect the redemption of the human family and its "liberation" from every oppressive situation. To me, that's the Magna Charta [of contemporary Catholicism].[26]

This concern for justice was confirmed and reiterated in the 1974 Synod on Evangelization and in subsequent regional conferences. In the words of Gutierrez, "the God of biblical revelation is known through interhuman justice. When justice does not exist, God is not known."[27]

The Church and the Poor

The biblical motif that has been most prominent in the years since 1980 is that of the poor and of the church's calling to bring good news to the poor. Self-evidently connected to the preceding motifs, the focus on the poor begins with the rediscovery of the attention given to the poor in the Bible. It is informed by the prophetic concern for the poor and nourished by Jesus' expressed commitment to bring good news to the poor. It was a disconcerting discovery to learn that many of the leading characters, and certainly much in the biblical environment, reflect a situation of poverty.

Concern for the poor has never been absent from the church's mission understanding, but it has gained new force through the eyes of Third World persons involved in ministry with the poor. Particularly significant have been the meetings of the conference of bishops of Latin America (CELAM), in Medellin, Colombia, in 1968 and Puebla, Mexico, in 1979. Those conferences confidently noted that in the concrete life situations God takes the side of the poor, and called the church (and committed the Latin American church) to exercise "a preferential option for the poor."[28] The CELAM conferences have had a galvanizing effect upon the church in Latin America, giving impetus to liberation theology, and affecting the thinking of those concerned for mission everywhere.

Among Protestants the concern for the poor found clear focus in Melbourne in 1980 at the missionary conference of the Commission on World Mission and Evangelism. Organized under the theme of Jesus' prayer, "Your Kingdom Come," the conference found that thinking about God's kingdom inevitably led to concern for the poor of the earth. In Bible study the participants learned again of God's special concern for the poor as this was clearly expressed in Jesus' ministry. They came to agree, as had the bishops of CELAM, that poverty is neither God's will nor fate, but the product of human systems and decisions. Under the guidance of Raymond Fung, a lay theologian then working with industrial laborers in Hong Kong and now in the office of evangelism of the World Council of Churches, they came to understand the poor to be "sinned against" as well as sinners. In his post-Melbourne editorial, Emilio Castro said:

> The second concentration point of Melbourne is the affirmation of the poor as the missiological principle par excellence. The relation to the poor inside the Church, outside the Church, nearby and far away, is the criterion to judge the authenticity and credibility of the Church's missionary engagement.[29]

In January 1982, the conference of the International Association of Mission Studies in Bangalore, India, also found it necessary to give attention to the challenge posed by the poor for the mission of the church. In recent years there have been many studies on the subject, ranging from treatments of the biblical understanding of the poor to concrete suggestions for the church in mission.[30] Of special interest have been studies describing social and economic conditions in the biblical settings and in the world of the early Christians.[31] The general consensus of mission thinking is that God's concern for all people finds special expression in God's concern for poor and oppressed people, and that a special concern of the church in mission must be to take sides with, or to be in solidarity with, the poor.[32] Such a mission focus inevitably draws the church to go beyond charity for the poor—even almsgiving in the Old Testament was a matter of justice, not of charity—and to ask whether concrete actions can be taken to change the systems which produce and perpetuate poverty. That conviction leads the church into advocacy and into efforts for liberation of the poor, activities which are held to be consistent with both Luke 4:18ff. and Matt. 25:31-44. This conclusion becomes inescapable when it is seen that in the biblical understanding poverty is inseparable from oppression.[33] In a *Working Paper on Mission,* received by the 1984 Budapest Assembly of the Lutheran World Federation and soon to be published for study and comment by the church bodies, paragraph 53 asserts:

> Today we need to address more strongly the underlying causes of poverty and injustice, and to develop more faithful missionary actions accordingly. We call upon our churches to develop as a central priority programs and approaches which seek to respond to the overwhelming reality of poverty and injustice in our time, and to do this both as individual churches and as churches gathered for joint mission.

Kingdom of God

The fifth biblical motif that has energized contemporary mission thinking is that of the kingdom of God. This is an old and well-known motif. Scholars agree that this motif was dominant in the teaching and ministry of Jesus.

> The central aspect of the teaching of Jesus was that concerning the kingdom of God. Of this there can be no doubt and today no scholar does, in fact, doubt it.[34]

Although the kingdom motif has always been part of missiological thinking it was frequently relegated to the closet of a totally futuristic eschatology, as something "not of this world" and therefore not especially helpful to the church. This could be done, of course, only by ignoring the fact that in the New Testament the kingdom was considered to be *both* present *and* future, and that kingdom preaching is prominent in early Christian thinking, as a reading of Acts, Revelation, 1 Peter, or Hebrews will show. In the minds of many, however, the balance tilted in the other direction when the social gospel movement too readily identified the kingdom with the efforts of Christians whose mission aim was to bring in the kingdom.

After remaining dormant for some decades, the kingdom motif is again asserting its powerful influence on mission thinking. It was not given much attention at Lausanne, but that "tremendous flow in evangelical theology" was the subject of some comment. Orlando Costas reports that Michael Green said at Lausanne:

> How much have we heard here about the kingdom of God? Not much. It is not our language. But it was Jesus' prime concern. He came to show that God's kingly rule had broken into our world; it no longer lay entirely in the future, but was partly realized in him and those who followed him. The Good News of the kingdom was both preached by Jesus and embodied by him. . . . So it must be with us.[35]

At the meeting of the Commission on World Mission and Evangelism in Melbourne, however, the theme "Your Kingdom Come" insured that careful attention would be given to the kingdom motif from a mission perspective. The insights of Melbourne have been appropriated widely. Melbourne understood the kingdom to be eschatological in character, to be both future in its fullness yet present in incomplete power. It understood *kingdom* to refer to the rule or reign of God, and therefore to be related to the mission task of proclaiming and embodying God's rule in the entire creation. It did not envision the church's bringing in the kingdom or establishing it. It understood that to announce that the kingdom of God is at hand is to provide "a challenge to repent and an invitation to believe."[36]

Melbourne saw the function of the church as that of a sign of the kingdom, a witness to God's Lordship over all that exists. This witness or signing function would be by both word and deed, so that the existence of the church as the body of Christ would itself bear witness. Thus significant attention must be paid to the internal life and activity of the church, not out of a maintenance mentality but in order to assure a faithful witness. Using language first developed in Roman Catholic mission thinking, Melbourne came to see the church as "a sacrament of the kingdom." In a sacramental way the church as Christ's body makes Christ really present in the world.

> This sacramental reality of the Church, which moved us so much in Melbourne, is fully manifested in the celebration of the Eucharist. The Eucharist is described as the pilgrim bread, missionary bread, food for a people on the march. . . . It is a foretaste of the kingdom which proclaims the Lord's death until he comes.[37]

A sign of the kingdom, the church is also called to be an instrument of the kingdom, "by continuing Christ's mission to the world in a struggle for the growth of all human beings into the fullness of life."[38] This instrumental role will mean the church will be engaged in God's struggles in the world. "In their witness to the kingdom of God in words and deeds the churches must dare to be present at the bleeding points of humanity and thus near those who suffer evil."[39]

In fidelity to its focus on the kingdom the church will also find itself examining and confronting the structures and organizations of the world.

> In the prayer our Lord gave to his Church we are encouraged to pray in solidarity with all peoples for the coming of God's kingly rule, and that God's will be done on earth as it is in heaven. In the light of this we realize that the structures of our societies—whether religious, political or economic—have become hindrances . . . or have actively repressed or even prevented the development of women and men into the fullness of life, thereby denying people their God-given right to dignity and growth.[40]

The motif of the kingdom provides rich resources for learning and growing in mission, and has stimulated mission thinking around the world. As Castro puts it,

> today it would be difficult to come across a theological search for missionary clarity that is not conducted from the perspective of a kingdom theology. Practically all contextual theologies of the Third World attempt to interpret reality—historical, cultural and political—in terms of visions of the future within a kingdom perspective.[41]

Idolatry

A sixth biblical motif that is beginning to be significant in modern mission theology is that of God in struggle against false gods or idols. This is an ancient motif, sometimes mistakenly believed to belong to an earlier age and worldview. It has been treated very gently lest it be misused to signify the encounter of the Christian faith with adherents of other living faiths, but it is finding increasing value in analyzing the role of the church as it attempts to discharge its mission.

In the preceding section it was seen that to take seriously the kingdom motif brings the church into confrontation with those forces that resist the rule of God in the world. Frequently, however, those forces are the concrete expression of the principalities and powers against which God contends in every age. As one section report at Melbourne said,

> there is a temptation for the established leadership in the churches to avoid confrontation with the struggles of this world on the grounds that the kingdom of God is not "of this world." It is true that it is not of this world but it is "at hand" precisely in a confrontation with principalities and powers as has been clearly revealed to the churches in the life of Jesus Christ.[42]

In many ways God is engaged in a struggle for supremacy, "wrestling against those powers and forces which oppose his liberating and gracious authority."[43] The shape of those forces is seen to be different today than the Baalim and Ashtaroth of the Old Testament, but their power is fearsome. The idols are human creations raised to a position of ultimacy and demanding allegiance that properly belongs only to God. The struggle is aptly described in the title of a recent book by Pablo Richard and other Latin American theologians, *The Idols of Death and the God of Life*. José Comblin describes the struggle with one such idol in *The Church and the National Security State*, published by Orbis. These contemporary idols or false gods take many forms.

> Such modern idols as totalitarian regimes, whether Nazi or Stalinist; racial supremacy myths, whether South African or American; the national security state, of left or right; the ultimacy of military power, whether nuclear or conventional; loyalty to a particular economic system, whether capitalist or Leninist; the coercive power of money or of human laws or of social conformity—all these are idols as surely as if they were carved from cedar or garnished with gold.[44]

The mission implication of the motif of the battle against the gods is that the church is called to challenge the claims of the false gods and to resist the damaging effects of their claims on human lives. A simple witness to the kingdom of God, the Lordship of Christ, will itself constitute such a challenge, but the church is called even more directly to confront those pretenders to divinity, to proclaim "God's judgment upon any authority, power or force, which would openly or by subtle means deny people their full human rights."[45]

Cross and Suffering

That brings us directly to the final biblical motif in modern mission theology, namely, that of the cross. Contemporary missiology understands that the church inherits Christ's mission (John 20:21) and that it may well inherit the suffering that accompanied Christ's mission.

> And if we do these things, uphold the faith and hope of God's people, . . . then we must not be surprised that suffering will come to many of our brothers and sisters. And it is almost the other side of the coin to witnessing. It is no accident that the Greek word for *witness* is the one we have taken over as *martyr.*[46]

The experience of Christians in many parts of the world has brought to critical consciousness the connection between mission and suffering. It could hardly be otherwise. If the Christian mission involves witnessing to the liberating power of the God who is concerned for the poor and oppressed, and involves challenging the idols of a still powerful realm, then suffering is an obvious consequence of Christian mission. And in our age, the list of martyrs grows alarmingly. Yet as Christians bury their martyrs they are renewed to the calling that leads to a cross.

> The churches must dare to be present at the bleeding points. . ., even taking the risk of being counted among the wicked. The royal reign of God appears on earth as the kingdom of the crucified Jesus, which places his disciples with him under the cross.[47]

With full consciousness that the words are not empty phrases, but are abstract references to concrete cases of persons bleeding and dying under torture, mission thinkers continue to aver that "our mission above all will have a heightened concern for ministry under the sign of the cross."[48] "Credible and authentic mission in our world cannot take place without Christian discipleship and cross-bearing."[49] Mission theology, under the motif of the cross, calls the church to move forward into encounter with a frequently hostile world, bearing a message forged in suffering and death, yet shining with hope and life, knowing that the Christian church in mission may be called to tread the same path as the Lord who commissions it.

In summary: There has been a hermeneutical revolution in the theology of mission. The insights and experiences of Christians in the Third World have both challenged the formerly prevailing assumptions and have shed new light on the biblical witness. Four overarching themes were identified, themes which persist in all the biblical motifs, shaping and conforming them (God active in history; God active through human agents; hope; and universality of mission). Seven out of many biblical motifs were identified as being of particular significance for the development of mission theology in recent years and in the foreseeable future (liberation, justice, salvation, good news to the poor, the kingdom of God, true God versus false gods, and suffering and the cross).

PART II

BIBLE AND MISSION IN THE CONGREGATION

7

BIBLE AND MISSION IN AN INNER-CITY CONGREGATION

Barbara Jurgensen

How We Reactivated Our Inner-City Congregation

Susan was a small, dark-haired girl of 12. Her father had been struck down and robbed one evening as he was taking out the garbage, and never regained consciousness. Now, a few months later, Susan and her mother had moved to the neighborhood of our church.

When I visited their apartment, above a grocery store, one afternoon, I asked Susan if she was in a Sunday school.

"I've never been to Sunday school," she said.

When I learned she was about to start seventh grade, I invited her to come also to confirmation class. And she did. She knew none of the Bible stories. We were the first to tell her about Jesus coming to earth as a baby, about his love for us and his giving of his life, about his calling us to follow him.

Susan came early to class each week to clean the chalkboard and get the workbooks spread out on the table. She stayed after class to make sure everything was put away. Through the Bible stories we focused on week by week, Susan found that she had a Lord who loved her.

Susan was one of many unchurched young people we brought in from our inner-city neighborhood who came to know Jesus through the people of our congregation and the pages of God's Word.

When I began serving as pastor at First Lutheran Church, about four miles northwest of downtown Chicago, the people's first concern in August that year was to get the confirmation class going.

People expected the church to close in a few months; when the neighborhood changed the congregation lost nine-tenths of its members in a flight to the suburbs. Some said the congregation once had 1200 members, some said as many as 1500. Now it was down to around 170, and most of them were older, retired people. How could they maintain a church building that seated almost 500?

But they wanted to get the confirmation class going before the two families that had children in that age group (two in each) decided to go elsewhere. They were pleased to have a class of four that year, but I said, "That's not enough. There must be a lot of unchurched seventh and eighth graders in this neighborhood. Why don't you look around for kids living in the houses on either side of you and across the street and in your apartment building. Bring me their names, then you invite them and I'll invite them."

Each Sunday I reminded them of this during the announcements, and by the time we started confirmation class in early October we had our own 4 plus 6 unchurched young people from the neighborhood. The people kept bringing names and I kept visiting them; by Christmas we had 15 in the confirmation class.

It was a challenge to try to relate the Bible story to 11 students who knew almost nothing about it. Some were puzzled by it, some suspicious, some seemingly unconcerned, but some became very interested in learning more.

Ken, a well-muscled kid who tried to act tough, said to me one day after class, "Jesus probably doesn't want to know people who've done bad things, right? He just wants to know good people. . . ."

"Just the opposite," I assured him. "He came especially for people who've been through a lot of hard times and done things they shouldn't have and really need him."

Life in Our Neighborhood Wasn't Easy for Kids

A number of these kids had older brothers who were gang members, and some of them in a few years would probably be gang members themselves. They came to class talking about a classmate who had freaked out on drugs that day or who had gotten beat up by a rival gang, or who was in trouble with the law.

Life was not the easiest for a kid in this neighborhood, but it also sharpened their choices. They couldn't just drift along—to drift along was to go downhill fast. The neighborhood had 22 gangs, the most of any neighborhood in the city of Chicago, and also the highest incidence of gang-related crime.

When I came to work one Monday morning after spending the weekend downstate at a convention, the custodian reported that there had been two boys killed by gangs Saturday night, one shot less than 60 feet from the parish house and another hanged in a gangway halfway down the block.

How do you bring our Lord to kids living in such a situation?

We began by reading the Bible stories in the Old and New Testaments. Then we retold them in modern language: "Jesus was walking down Fullerton Avenue late one night when he saw a man who had been stabbed lying in the gangway between the dental lab and the tire shop. . . ." So began our version of the story of the good Samaritan. And we acted the stories out, one of their favorite activities. One end of the classroom was our impromptu stage, and most of them liked to get up and act out the story as it might happen today.

We had "spelldowns" on the Bible stories they'd already learned. We turned some of the stories into songs. I got out my three-stringed ukulele (I never did get around to getting the broken string replaced) and we sang our way through the Bible, making up songs as we went.

Let's Do the Same with Our Sunday School

After Christmas the people of the congregation said, "Why don't we try to do the same thing with our Sunday school that we did with the confirmation class?"

So, during announcements each Sunday, I'd ask the people to look around their neighborhood for children of Sunday school age, and not to just *invite* them but to *bring* them on Sunday.

Our Sunday school had 18 children enrolled that fall, but several families had moved so far away that they rarely got there. Only 9 of the children were regular attenders. In the early fall the teachers said, "Well, it looks like we're about ready to fold up." After Christmas they said, "Let's get busy and build the Sunday school up like we did the confirmation class."

The Sunday school had had a system of awarding a pin at the end of the school year for perfect attendance. But we decided children who had never been to Sunday school before needed a more immediate award, so we began offering a lapel pin—a dove or a fish as Christian symbols—for just 10 Sundays of attendance.

We also started having free pancake breakfasts half an hour before Sunday school to which children could bring their friends on the first Sunday of every month. We awarded a foreign coin to each child who brought an unchurched child to Sunday school. One of our members contributed an ornate metal box and coins from many countries.

When he installed me, our bishop had remarked that if he were in a parish he would like to try telling the story of the Bible to the Sunday school in a continuous way. I began for about five minutes each Sunday during the opening of Sunday school, starting with Abraham and Sarah, and got as far as the second battle of Ai by June. They seemed to enjoy it and I learned a lot. Some of the teachers said they appreciated hearing the Bible story put together as one related whole.

So we emphasized the Bible stories. And our Sunday school grew so that by the end of the school year we had about 25 regular attenders. It was then that the people began to realize that the church wasn't going to close. "We can *do* it!" they told each other. "We've built up the confirmation class and the Sunday school and now we can build up the church as well."

Let's Bring the Bible to Our Adult Members

Joe Sittler once suggested that at least once a year a congregation devote sermon time for a month to the study of a particular book of the Bible. Our records showed that January was our lowest month for church attendance. So we decided to look at the book of Philippians together—there were four Sundays and four chapters.

In November we began publicizing the upcoming event. In our monthly newsletters we started giving a background on the book of Philippians and urged people to begin reading it and thinking about it. In our weekly church bulletins we kept adding pieces of information that would help us understand Paul and the situation at Philippi.

We encouraged people to bring their own Bibles but also provided New Testaments in the pews. We also encouraged them to tell neighbors, relatives, and friends about our upcoming series and to pick them up and bring them along.

January came and we had a tremendously good turnout. We did about 20 minutes of Bible study together during our usual sermon time, and a number of people asked if we could do it again that year, so we selected August, our second-lowest month for attendance, and did the five chapters of 1 Thessalonians on the five Sundays, again with very good attendance. January and August thereafter became our Bible study months, and we focused first on the books with four or five chapters: Colossians, 2 Timothy, Ruth, 1 John, Lamentations, 1 Peter, James, Jonah, and Malachi.

There are also a number of books with three or six chapters (Galatians, Ephesians, 2 Thessalonians, 1 Timothy, Joel, 2 Peter, Titus, Nahum, Habakkuk, and Zephaniah) that could be divided to fit the Sundays. And there are smaller books (Philemon, 2 John, 3 John, Jude) that could be studied together. There are longer books that could be studied in part, or in a more sweeping manner.

The first three years I was in the parish I decided to preach each Sunday on the Old Testament lesson (with references to the gospel and epistle) to give us more understanding of that less familiar part of God's Word. I could then use these stories as illustrations in later sermons and thus reinforce the learning experience.

I found that Bible stories of all kinds can enhance the sermon. We need to hear not only stories from today and stories from the preacher's experience but stories from God's Word, stories to ponder, stories that can act like radiation implants, informing our thoughts and attitudes and actions as we live our days.

I found out that children's sermons can be made more lively by frequent use of stories from the Bible. Children especially enjoy hearing about what Jesus said and did. Whenever I began a children's sermon by saying, "One day Jesus. . .," I could see their attention pick up.

Let's Involve Everyone in the Work of Our Congregation

We had an unusual number of older people and home-bound members in our parish. When most of the younger and middle-aged people moved out of the neighborhood as it began changing, many of the older people said, "This has always been our home and we're not going to leave." And they didn't. So we had 50 people in church on a typical Sunday (which grew gradually to 60, 70, 80, 90), and there were about 15-20 home-bound members who needed regular visits.

One of our elderly women, who had become quite disabled, said to me one day, "I'm not much good for anything any more. I can't work at church, I can't even attend church, and I can't give very much."

I replied, "But could you pray for our congregation and the work our Lord is calling it to do? Could you do that every day?"

She said she could and would. Each time I visited her after that she told me that she never missed a day. Several others who were home-bound agreed to do the same.

Some of those who were home-bound liked to discuss the sermon texts for the coming Sunday with me. This became their way of having some input, of making a contribution to the life and work of the congregation. I appreciated their sharing some of their life stories, called to remembrance by the text, and sometimes with their permission incorporated their stories into the sermon the following Sunday.

Let's Help Our Vacation Bible School Grow

As our first educational year was coming to an end and we were getting ready to close down Sunday school and confirmation class for the summer, it was time to plan for vacation Bible school. We decided to hold our VBS in August when the children were beginning to look for something to do and when we might be able to interest them in starting Sunday school with us a few weeks later.

At our planning meeting one of the teachers said, "If we don't have more than 20 children this year, I think we should stop having VBS. It's too much work getting ready for so few kids."

They had been holding their VBS jointly with a church four or five blocks away, and their combined attendance usually was between 15 and 20.

"Twenty kids!" I said. "There are a lot more than 20 kids living right in this block!" On each side of our street were about 10 two-flats, and some of these buildings also had apartments in the basement and on the third floor. So there had to be at least 50 families right in our block, and many of them were young families with children. On nice days there would often be a dozen or more children out playing along the sidwalks.

"How about some of the neighborhood kids?" I asked.

"They never come," they replied.

"Well, why don't we go out and invite them?" I suggested. I looked around the fellowship hall, which was our only space for classes. "How many kids do you think we could handle?"

We decided on six classes of 10 students each, since 10 could sit around each of our big tables. Then we drew up some registration sheets with room for 10 names in each class and the next two days a couple of us went out door to door. In about three hours of visiting we filled all the classes and had to put some younger children on a waiting list.

When the other church saw the kind of registration we had achieved, they decided to do the same thing in their neighborhood, and from then on we each held a well-attended VBS.

Vacation Bible school became an occasion for getting some of the parents of the children into the church. On the Thursday evening of VBS week we planned a program with the kids singing songs they'd learned, telling Bible stories, and exhibiting the things they'd made. Usually at least half of them got their parents to come and it gave us a good chance to begin getting acquainted.

Each year we made a special effort to encourage these new children to continue on with Sunday school.

A Little Child Shall Lead Them

After we had been doing all these things for a few years and could reflect back, we could see that it was mainly through our children's and youth activities that we were bringing new families into the church. It started with the kids coming to confirmation class, Sunday school, or VBS. Then the parents came to see their children taking part in the VBS or Sunday school program, or in Confirmation Participation Sunday, which was a special day we invented for one Sunday each spring and each fall when every student in our confirmation class had a special part in the Sunday morning worship.

Some read parts of the lessons or prayers, others served as acolytes, ushers, or choir members. Parents received special invitations to be present and were asked to provide cookies for the coffee hour following the service. Usually at least half of them came.

"A little child shall lead them" gained a new meaning in our congregation. It was as we reached out into the neighborhood and brought in unchurched children and then encouraged their parents to come and see what they were doing that our church began to grow. Now we needed to have a new-member class two and sometimes three times a year to begin incorporating the parents.

Council, Camp, and Reaching Out

We also found the study of the Bible to be an important part of our church council meetings. When I first started work at the church, the agenda for the meetings called for opening devotions by the pastor, then the business and committee reports, then, last of all, the pastor's report. I soon found that in the 10 minutes or so allowed for my report at the end of the meeting I could not do the job I wanted to do. So instead I selected some area of our congregation's or the wider church's ministry to focus on each month, found a Scripture passage underscoring such action, and turned the opening devotional period into a time of studying the Word and seeing what our Lord might be calling us to do and be in our particular time and place.

This set our council meeting into a framework of exploring what our Lord might be asking us to do rather than just seeing what items of business needed to be attended to.

Bible camp also became an important part of our life as a congregation. Once, during the first winter I was there, we were sitting around the table at confirmation class, watching yet more snow pile up along our street. It seemed like a good time to introduce the idea of Bible camp.

"Have any of you ever been to Bible camp?" I asked. None had. "What is it?" they wanted to know.

"Well," I said, "You live in cabins and go hiking through the woods and swimming and canoeing—and you meet new kids—and have Bible studies—and eat outdoors. . . ."

"How much does it cost?" they wanted to know. When I said that it was $65, they said, "No way. Our moms don't have $65."

That I already knew. Most of their families would be hard pressed just to give them a little spending money for the week.

"Don't worry," I said. "We're all going to go. Everyone that's willing to work, that is. We can have car washes and bake sales, we can rake yards and shovel snow. . . ."

"We could shovel snow today," someone suggested. Several groaned, but they began making plans.

And so we worked all that late winter and spring, and by the time June arrived we had earned more than enough money to take 10 kids who worked and wanted to go to camp. For some of them it was the only time they got out of the city of Chicago. To get to pile into a van and head for a woodsy camp two hours north into Wisconsin was almost beyond their wildest dreams.

Bible camp became an important part of our youth work.

So our congregation grew and became more active. We opened a food pantry for those in need in our neighborhood, and later a clothing "pantry." We began having a children's procession down our street on Christmas Eve, Las Posadas, to bring in a tradition of the Hispanics who were becoming more numerous in our neighborhood.

We made banners and we ate spaghetti together. We made occasions to get to know each other, to bring friends, to invite in our neighbors.

And at the center was our Lord and his love for us. It was he who was working all the time through us, calling his people to himself and sending them out to be his people in the world. It is, after all, his world. He made it and was working in it long before we came along. He created his world by his Word in order that he might do his redeeming work in us and in all people. And he invites us to join him in this work everywhere—even in the inner city.

8

BIBLE AND MISSION IN A LARGE CONGREGATION

Lowell O. Larson

More than Size

There are, of course, many factors in addition to size that affect the understanding and experience of mission in any congregation. There are enough similarities in the faith and life of all Christian churches to assure that mission will also be similar among them. At the same time, among congregations of similar size there can be enough different influences at work to make it impossible for any one of them to be, in every respect, representative of all.

Some Other Features

It seems important to me, then, to begin this report with an attempt to identify some distinguishing features of the life and faith of the congregation I serve, features which it shares with many others, but not with all.

It has a long history, having been founded 118 years ago, in a comparatively stable community and region in central Minnesota. The region is largely agricultural but, with a number of attractive lakes, it has also become an area for leisure and recreational activity and for retirement living. The community is a regional center of 18,000 residents with a community college and an area vocational-technical institute, a state hospital for the chemically dependent, the mentally retarded, and the mentally ill, several group homes, a regional "community services" center, a large "sheltered workshop," a general hospital and a medical clinic that serve a wide area, a regional office of Lutheran Social Services, the headquarters of a district of the American Lutheran Church and a region of the Presbyterian Church, U.S.A. Both the region and the community are heavily churched. There are 24 churches in the town, 5 of them Lutheran.

Including "Convictions"

A number of rather traditional convictions (assumptions?) about Bible and mission in the church have, in my judgment, been widely shared in our congregation, by both members and staff. One is that the right use of the Bible is itself the central mission of the church! Implied here is the further assumption, perhaps not as often expressed, that the true mission of the church is in reality the mission of God, who accomplishes it by the Word witnessed and communicated in the Bible. The Word is a "means of grace," and the first business of the church is to proclaim it. The church is to "administer" the Bible "in accordance with the gospel."[1] When it does, God is able to accomplish the *missio Dei* in and through the church.

This means that worship is also a basic part of the church's mission: *Gottesdienst,* God's service to us and our service and witness to one another and to the world and, as such, our service as well to God. There would be widespread agreement among us, I believe, with assertions like those of Peter Taylor Forsyth: "The greatest product of the church is not brotherly love but divine worship,"[2] and of William Willimon: "There may be no better answer, or solution (to the problem of 'resistance') than to simply continue to praise God and ask for grace."[3]

In worship and in the faithful preaching and teaching of the message of the Bible, seeds are planted that can be counted on to produce the fruits of faith and love, when and where God pleases.[4] The Word "takes hold of one today and falls into his heart, tomorrow it touches another, and so on. Thus quietly and soberly it will do its work, and no one will know how it all came about."[5]

The calling and gathering of a fellowship of believers, the creation of the church—as it *is,* justified by grace and not by works—is part of the mission of God. The church *is* (not "shall become") the "body of Christ."[6] Therefore, love and concern for one another in the church, the church's upbuilding of itself in love (Eph. 4:16), is an indispensable part of the church's own mission.

The church, in turn, is thus enabled to love the world and to care for the earth. We do this together as a community of faith, in league with other such communities, in worship and proclamation and teaching and in deeds of compassion and service. However, the "setting of daily life [is] the primary arena for the exercise of Christian calling."[7] "Christian love and genuine good works" are normally manifested in one's "station of life," according to one's "own calling" in the secular realm.[8]

In the Center, Worship

The centrality of worship for the mission of the church is uniquely symbolized in our congregation by the design of its buildings, intended by architect and members as a visual theological statement. A round sanctuary is set in the center of a "square" bounded by units for education and fellowship, amid four courtyards, representing the world, visible through stained glass window-walls in which all of the colors of the prism are used in fluid forms to suggest the ongoing creative activity of God. A band of red encircling the sanctuary (the only unbroken line) is identified as a symbol of the movement of the Spirit of God who calls and gathers the church. Above the glass is another circle of oak panels on which are carved the words from Hebrews 12: "Therefore, since we are surrounded by so great a cloud of witnesses, let us also lay aside every weight, and sin which clings so closely, and let us run with perseverance the race that is set before us, looking to Jesus the pioneer and perfecter of our faith. . . ." Above this Bible passage are painted the names of representative witnesses from the Old and New Testament eras and from the history of the church, concluding with such near contemporaries as Berggrav, Bonhoeffer, and Ordass, and finally, with two blank spaces for those who will "follow in their train."

The congregation is gathered in semicircular fashion around the pulpit, table, and font. Preaching has always been considered important in this congregation and care is taken to attempt to convey the message of the biblical texts, almost always from the lectionary, "in accordance with the gospel," with the promise of the new life it conveys and the judgment it reveals upon the old.

With the use of *Lutheran Book of Worship* we have participated in renewed appreciation of Baptism and its significance for both the life and the mission of the church. Consideration is being given to better ways of preparing and supporting families and candidates and sponsors.

For the last three years the table has become as central in our practice as it is by its physical presence, as we have begun to serve communion, except on rare occasions, at every Sunday morning worship service. Over a year was spent in study and preparation for this change, beginning with a district communion forum, continuing with a Sunday morning Lenten series of sermons (the practice was begun on Easter Sunday) and study in our own "forums" and in sessions of the worship committee, the altar guild, and the church council. We made extensive use of "A Statement on Communion Practices" issued jointly in 1978 by the American Lutheran Church and the Lutheran Church in America, which states, "The earliest Lutheran practice provides an appropriate goal for the frequency of the full service of Word and Sacrament. 'In our churches Mass is celebrated every Sunday and on other festivals when the Sacrament is offered to those who wish for it. . .' (Apol. 24.1). Congregations are encouraged to move toward this goal because the complete service of Holy Communion embodies the fullness of the Means of Grace, because it provides an excellent focus for the whole Christian life and mission, and because it witnesses to our confessional and ecumenical heritage."

Communion has also been made available among us to younger children, below fifth grade, whose parents will participate with them in preparation. Plans are under way to have the sacrament brought by assisting ministers directly from the table to home-bound parishioners who may then receive it as they worship with the congregation by their radios.

Many of us have come to see communion not only as "comfort for terrified consciences"[9] but as "precious food for missionaries, bread and wine for pilgrims on their apostolic journey."[10] It not only "awakens faith"[11] but "embraces all aspects of life" and "demands reconciliation and sharing among all those regarded as brothers and sisters in the one family of God and is a constant challenge in the search for appropriate relationships in social, economic and political life."[12]

One advantage of a large congregation is that its mission of worship can reach more people. This outreach has been extended among us by a radio broadcast of Sunday morning worship that has been on the air continuously for 47 years.

Surrounded by Teaching

In the best Lutheran tradition, our congregation has always been very aware of its mission to teach the Bible and its meaning for faith and life. Another advantage of its size is that a staff member can have education as a major responsibility. Public schools in this community still release pupils for an hour a week for religious instruction and, in addition to Sunday school for all ages, we have "released time" classes for pupils in grades three through nine.

Education for children has increasingly been supplemented by education for adults. In addition to the familiar monthly studies in women's circles and to periodic short courses, the Bethel Bible Series has been used, and, now, the SEARCH Weekly Bible Studies prepared by the American Lutheran Church. Various studies in theology have been offered, including courses on the Lutheran Confessions and on the *Evangelical Catechism.* "Current issue" forums seek to help make connections among faith and life and mission.

Upbuilding in Love

The nurture of members and the care of the church as a body are considered among us to be an essential mission of the congregation, biblically mandated. I personally fear some danger to the church, and so to the mission of the church, from emphases on "mission" that seem to assume that all church members are, or should be, always ready and able to "serve" in all sorts of enterprises, and that almost seems to value the church primarily as a source of personnel and money for programs and projects. Actually, all of us need also to be served and there are times when all we have to bring to the church is that need. We are, as Luther saw at the end, "beggars." Sometimes we cannot even praise God: all we can do is ask for grace!

The care of the church begins with regard for the church as it is, quite apart from what it can do. The nurture of people, including people in the church, begins with regard for them as they are, with all their needs, including the need for forgiveness.

> A living body of Christ has *always* had two foci, itself and the world. We ought to have discovered this from our study of the Pauline writings. Paul's concern is twofold. First, for that body which is dynamic and which has parts functioning together. This body pays attention to itself, appreciates and builds upon the contribution of all members. It cares, really cares, for all its members, feeding, supporting, and sustaining those diverse parts. It is self-directed and raises critical questions about its parts and how they function. It is involved in personal crises. Any personal crisis is a threat to the whole body and the functioning of the body as the body of Christ.[13]

Concern for the mission of the congregation to feed and tend the flock and to love one another has issued among us recently in the formation, in consultation with Lutheran Social Services, of a parish care team. This team has among its objectives enabling the congregation "faithfully and creatively [to] respond to and meet the needs of our parishioners. (We want to be a congregation of warmth and compassion and provide opportunities for growth)." The team has worked to date with existing committees, the council and auxiliary groups, offering encouragement and training to pay attention to relationships, along with programs and tasks. (A parish personnel relations committee relates specifically to staff with similar objectives.)

Another objective of the parish care team is to provide "opportunities and training" for the cultivation and sharing of talents in ministry by members of the congregation. The mission of the church to care for its members and for the "body" includes respecting the gifts that people have been given, enabling them to "discern and exercise" those gifts, and providing "structures and processes of decision making that will foster mutuality and the participation of those affected by the decisions."[14] Our congregation is governed by a church council which works through 13 standing committees on which other members also serve and which are given both responsibility and authority—committees on education of children and youth, education of adults, fellowship, "life and growth," missions, property improvement, property maintenance, public relations, social concerns, stewardship, worship, and youth involvement. Members are also involved in the work of the congregation in many other ways, of course: as teachers, as assisting ministers at worship, as visitors of those who are ill and home-bound, as advisors and chaperons for youth, as officers and workers in auxiliary organizations, etc. Training is now being planned to equip members for one-to-one "caring ministry" and for facilitation of groups for support and for growth.

We try to respect and value the *diversity* of gifts and experiences and perspectives of members of the congregation. We do not strive to be "homogeneous," but rather to be representative of the community. We attempt to make room for differing political, social, and economic views and for theological discussion (within the confessional context of justification by grace through faith). We encourage the exchange of views and try to deal with conflict honestly and constructively. We were able to "work through" the divorce and remarriage of a pastor by openly inviting the airing of dissent and providing the study of "ethical decision making" in a manner that preserved the unity of the congregation and the ministry of the pastor and affirmed him as a person.

Focus on the World

The primary way in which our congregation is in mission in the world is through our members in their callings in the setting of daily life. In addition to the usual necessary economic tasks, our parishioners are engaged in government and law, education, health care, social services, counseling, etc. We recognize and affirm that from time to time in preaching and in worship. We plan to provide more support and help for people to see and experience their vocations as Christian ministry and mission and I anticipate that this will receive attention from the parish care team.

The primary way in which our congregation is *collectively* engaged in mission in the world is in partnership with other congregations in our denomination and district and other associations. Again, I sense a danger to the church and to its mission in an emphasis on local initiative and control that could lead to further erosion of established strong and effective cooperative mission. Our congregation has consistently given high, "off the top" priority to its support of the mission of the larger church in its "benevolence" giving to denomination and district (including Lutheran Social Services) and in its participation in special appeals, such as those for college and seminary education and for "united mission." We partially support missionaries in South Africa. We regularly receive offerings for special "mission" causes such as the ALC Hunger Program and Lutheran World Relief, Lutheran Vespers and "50 More in '84." Endowment gifts by members enable us to provide some assistance to students in American Lutheran colleges and to persons preparing for ministry in the church. We join with conference churches in giving major support to campus ministry in our area. Many members participate—with congregational encouragement—in movements like Bread for the World and the Lutheran Human Relations Association. There is a lively and growing concern with the issues of peace and American policy in Central America.

Locally, our congregation has sponsored the resettlement of refugees—a Latvian family after World War II and two extended Vietnamese families in recent years—and has given them both ongoing support and the freedom to make their own decisions and to move on. We have cooperated with other Lutheran congregations to develop a joint program to help couples prepare for marriage and with other churches and groups in the community to establish a local "food shelf." We provide space in our buildings at cost for a preschool and for a day care and treatment center for the elderly. We furnish a meeting place for many community groups, church-related and others.

Focus on the Future

I sense a growing interest in our midst in strengthening our mission of witness and service. We are in the process of calling a pastor to assume primary responsibility for "life and growth," to include, along with nurture, such outreach. A "vision" study group spent several weeks evaluating current programs and projecting possibilities for expanded service, including sponsorship of an international student at a seminary, additional missionary support, partnership with a congregation with fewer resources, and additional training for lay ministry. Our church council is working on a mission statement and a new set of mission objectives.

Participation by one of our members in a national American Lutheran Church consultation on mission strategy has led to a proposal that we offer to undertake a pilot project for the synod to help develop a strategy for encouraging and enabling "each person and congregation to make mission a central factor in its . . . self-understanding as part of the church . . . [and to] 'lay claim to its turf.' " This would include further evaluation of the life and mission of the congregation now, a survey of community needs, determination of ways to assist persons and groups now responding to those needs or equipped to do so with help, exploration of possibilities for joint ministry with other churches, and, *only then,* consideration of new projects to be developed independently by the congregation.

As I write, we are in the process of preparing for a major stewardship emphasis to be directed by the Resident Stewardship Service of the American Lutheran Church in which Bible and mission will be very explicitly and practically related, and in which we hope to inspire commitments of support for increased witness and service.

Remembering (and rejoicing!) that we are justified by faith apart from the works of the law, we seek answers to the SEARCH question: "Given what God has done, what shape should the life of faith take?" We hope that we can also remember, amid all our goal-setting and strategizing, that we cannot dictate, and may not even be able to *know* ahead of time, what good works God has prepared, or will prepare, that we might walk in them,[15] and that it is the kingdom of *God* we are to serve and the will of *God* that is to be done. As we seek to relate Bible and mission to the ongoing life of the church, it is our hope that we can do so in the biblical spirit of the vespers prayer:

> Lord God, you have called your servants to ventures of which we cannot see the ending, by paths as yet untrodden, through perils unknown. Give us faith to go out with good courage, not knowing where we go, but only that your hand is leading us and your love supporting us; through Jesus Christ our Lord.[16]

9

BIBLE AND MISSION IN A HISPANIC CONGREGATION

Paul Collinson-Streng and Ismael de la Tejera

The Hispanic population of the United States is comprised of peoples from such widely diverse social, cultural, economic, and religious backgrounds that it would be impossible to speak in general terms of Bible and mission in a Hispanic congregation. Hispanics are a mosaic of different cultural, social, and religious shades, yet they are unified by one common feature: the Spanish language. In his essay "Towards an Hispanic Liturgy" Roberto Escamilla affirmed the unity of this diverse group.[1]

This essay will focus on mission with people of Mexican background who live in the Rio Grande Valley of south Texas, particularly the poor and migrant farm workers. We will describe our people historically, culturally, religiously, and economically in order to enhance the understanding of our context. We will then discuss the significance of the Bible for the newly converted and the significance of mission for the already converted. We will conclude by giving some recommendations and perspectives for mission which touch on current areas of debate.

I

This essay should not be understood as the result of a long commitment to evangelization within the Hispanic community. In our region we are just at the beginning of an evangelization process. It is only recently that the Lutheran church in our area, guided by the Holy Spirit, has become conscious of its prophetic and liberating mission, testifying of the good news to those who once "were no people but now are God's people" (1 Peter 2:10). We understand the concept of mission broadly, in a biblically holistic way. It is active proclamation of the gospel of Jesus Christ, of the coming of the kingdom of God, and of the call to become disciples, repenting of sin and living a life of faith.[2] We are interested in gathering groups together for the purposes of worship, Bible study, prayer and the sharing of Baptism and Holy Communion. We must both announce the good news and denounce that which is not in keeping with the coming kingdom.

We realize, without apology, that Hispanics are different from the immigrants to the 13 colonies, who had brought with them knowledge of the Bible. The cultural and religious backgrounds of Mexican-Americans in our region are products of both Spanish Catholicism and native Indian influences. In spite of the efforts of Protestant missionaries who have worked in Mexican territory for more than a century, there is still biblical illiteracy and little significant evangelization. The majority of the people we have contacted in this area had never read a Bible until recently, if at all.

Yet we must affirm, with Virgilio Elizondo, that "faith has always been a part of our culture, and culture has always been an instrument that manifests faith."[3] Religious history and popular opinion suggest that Mexican-Americans are primarily Roman Catholic; the truth, however, is that the religiosity of our people, in terms of Christian doctrine, is often very superficial. Popular Catholicism has often consisted of little more than making the sign of the cross and wearing religious medals. The people have been virtually ignorant of the Bible, in spite of the efforts of some Roman Catholic dioceses today. In our area, only seven miles from the Mexican border, the frame of reference for religious belief is often quite inadequate. For many of our people, religious doctrine is centered in devotion to the Virgin Mary. Our people do not realize that their popular religion contains many non-Christian elements. For example, the Cerro del Tepeyac, where the Virgin of Guadalupe appeared to the Indian Juan Diego, was previously the site of the temple of the Indian goddess Zihuacoatl (or Tonantzin, Indian Virgin Mother of the gods).

There are many popular beliefs and practices in the Rio Grande Valley that are a mixture of Christian belief and what might technically be called magic. An example is the continued popularity of *curanderismo,* a traditional healing system. If one has bad luck (*mala suerte*), suffers from the evil eye (*mal de ojo*) or has fright (*susto*), a visit to a *curandero* may be the only remedy. *Curanderos* are usually persons from the community who are like their patients, culturally and sociologically. They work on material, spiritual, and mental levels and are often recognized as having a "gift" for healing. Illnesses can have both natural and supernatural causes. The *curandero* can treat the supernatural causes with a mixture of objects such as eggs, lemons, garlic, candles, and oils (which are alleged to have intrinsic spiritual powers) and prayers, especially the Lord's Prayer or the Apostles' Creed. Some of the beliefs and practices are not limited to the lower social classes. Although many middle-class people say they do not believe in traditional practices they may still go through the actions. A personal friend who is a registered nurse was overheard by one of us repeating a special incantation after her four-year-old boy had fallen and cried at a birthday party.

Other interesting examples include the ways people try to influence God through vows and promises. For example, one might vow in a prayer to go on a religious pilgrimage or give a special offering if one is healed from sickness. When one of us asked a musician to play for a church service, he said that he had vowed to God that he would play for the church after he became famous, but he was not famous yet.[4]

Mexican-American popular piety is more clearly linked to the Roman church in the sacraments and the celebrations of the liturgical year. Baptism, marriage, and first communion seem to have a special significance for the people, as do Ash Wednesday and Holy Week celebrations.

Poverty also contributes to the continuation of prescientific worldviews. Our people are statistically the poorest of the poor in the United States; the official unemployment rate in Hidalgo County was more than 22% in February 1985. True unemployment, of course, is much higher. The average adult education level is from three to five years in the *colonias* (unincorporated rural communities) where we work. Most members live either in government subsidized housing or in wood-frame or concrete-block dwellings that they have constructed themselves. A significant number have outdoor toilets. When government and private institutions are also unresponsive to their needs, people conclude that they have no control over their own lives; God is viewed as the cause of some of the calamities of everyday life. For those in this culture of poverty, the Bible is God's book, and thus becomes a key for understanding the world.

One last comment on the religious situation is necessary. A large number of religious groups seek converts in the same areas and sometimes with less than friendly competition. Jehovah's Witnesses, Mormons, Seventh Day Adventists, Pentecostals and members of the Assemblies of God are all very active, and mainline Baptists and Methodists are also present. Roman Catholics have begun extensive lay training programs which are beginning to provide a new core of lay leadership. Each of these religious groups claims its authority on the basis of the Bible: church history, liturgical traditions, and ecumenical or Protestant confessions have little or no authority in this mission setting. Most of the sects are very critical of the Roman church and mainline Protestantism, holding that they do not teach biblical truth.

II

All of this leads us to a very necessary emphasis on the Bible. What significance does the Bible have for the newly converted? First, the Bible gives a sense of supernatural security and thus is received with profound respect. A great part of new converts' previous religious experience was filled with superstitions and non-Christian beliefs. Upon confronting the Bible, the newly converted person acquires the capability to transcend these limitations and to reflect upon human existence. The newly converted has a feeling of mystery, especially when dealing with God, of wanting to know more about the Spirit and the revelation of Jesus Christ as Savior. In addition to the blessings that the Word promises, the newly converted acquires an attitude of confidence and devotion towards the Bible and its promises. In some homes there will always be an opened Bible in some special place, a symbol of security, promise, and blessing. Some Pentecostal movements in this area use the Bible for healing purposes, touching the ill person's body with it.

Second, the Bible gives people dignity and power. In general, Hispanic people are characterized by these attitudes towards life: (1) an attitude of insecurity in terms of acceptance by new neighbors or fellow workers; (2) a search for love and understanding that will replace that left behind in their countries of origin; (3) a search for dignity and stability in the midst of a hostile society; (4) an expectation and hope for a change in their lives. The newly converted person, hearing the liberating message of the Bible, receives it as a message of dignity and power. In his or her life there is reaffirmed an individual identity characterized by the popular saying, "I am who I am, and I am like nobody else." This is because he or she has entered upon a personal relationship with God.

What does mission mean for the already converted? The first impression that the Hispanic mind has is that mission calls for responsibility, work, and resources. The Hispanic who is already converted feels inadequate when confronting these tasks: he can be responsible, if educated; he can learn new tasks, if taught; but when it comes to resources, he always feels limited. To the Hispanic, resources are understood in financial terms. The already converted, however, after serious confrontation with the message of the Scriptures, becomes a giver. The Hispanic becomes a person who gives because he or she is sure of the challenges, the promises, and the blessings that come with practicing that which is learned from the Bible. The giver who understands the significance of mission thus becomes a sustainer of the work of God.

There is also another change. As a result of a serious confrontation with the Scriptures, the already converted is transformed into an evangelist, a bearer of the good news. Accepting the biblical challenges "You shall be my witnesses in Jerusalem. . ." (Acts 1:8) and "Go therefore and make disciples of all nations. . ." (Matt. 28:19) the already converted becomes a subject of evangelization. His or her testimony is an expression of profound appreciation to God. Those who were no people have become God's people.

III

Perspectives and Recommendations for Mission among Hispanic People

1. Emphasize Bible and Spirit (Escaping our Cultural Ghetto)

Lutherans, as much as any Protestant denomination, have been prisoners in a sociological and cultural ghetto. We are primarily white, middle class, and of German or Scandinavian heritage. Our religious piety expresses this cultural baggage in our worship's liturgical style and emotional content. In extreme forms this means that being Lutheran involves using a particular book of worship, limited liturgical styles, and historic Lutheran hymns. An emphasis on the Bible and the biblical nature of our faith can give us the keys to escape this cultural ghetto.

Mission among low-income Mexican-American farm workers necessitates a biblical Lutheranism. Our liturgical tradition and culturally biased religious piety only get in our way as we reach out to these people. A Lutheran presence among poor farm workers does not mean translation of *Lutheran Book of Worship* into Spanish or teaching farm workers hymns from the German tradition. Neither does it imply teaching the historical Lutheran confessions, or perhaps even Luther's Small Catechism, except out of a historical interest for a selected few. Being Lutheran here rather implies a return to emphasis on the Bible as God's Word and the norm by which we judge and inform faith and life. Being Lutheran in this context means reading Paul to reach the conclusion of justification by faith, not just relying on Luther. Being Lutheran means reading the Exodus, the prophets, and the historical credo (Deut. 26:5-10) and applying them to today's situations of poverty and oppression. Being Lutheran implies reading the Bible and searching it for themes, such as the kingdom of God, which are central to the teaching of Jesus and the apostles and yet have been neglected by much of Protestant tradition. ("But when they believed Philip as he preached good news about the kingdom of God and the name of Jesus Christ, they were baptized, both men and women," Acts 8:12.) Being Lutheran in our context thus requires that we open ourselves to other cultures and that we give up much of our dependence on church history as we return to the Bible. It means overcoming a one-dimensional emphasis and spiritualization of the gospel which truncates the gospel, and returning to a biblical Christianity which announces good news to the poor.

Theological books, historical confessions, and much of our tradition must be judged in the light of a biblical faith. We read the Bible in small groups to grow in God's Word and find direction for our lives in some rather difficult situations. We pray for God's healing when we are sick and cannot afford to go to the doctor, and read of Jesus' miracles and promises to us. At the same time we struggle for that justice which is a central element of God's kingdom and convinces us that our members should also have the right to see the doctor when they need to and to be able to afford the medicines they need.

Where we will differ from so many of our Protestant brothers and sisters in this biblical emphasis is that God "has made us competent to be ministers of a new covenant, not in a written code but in the Spirit; for the written code kills, but the Spirit gives life" (2 Cor. 3:6). In our biblical emphasis we will not be so literalistic and fundamentalist, avoiding the bibliolatry of some of our evangelistic competitors. We search the Bible, not for laws to be followed, but for the gospel that gives life. Our methodology includes reflecting upon our reality in the light of the gospel, and then acting upon it.

Seventh Day Adventists, Jehovah's Witnesses, and other sectarian groups emphasize a particular understanding of, and particular parts of, the Bible as a way of demonstrating the biblical validity of their approach. We also can use this approach in a positive rather than in a negative manner so that we may gain peoples' attention and achieve credibility. As we teach people aspects of the biblical message of which they are not aware, we arouse their interest in the Christian faith as a whole.

2. *Start with People's Experience (Base Christian Communities)*

Successful mission necessitates starting with people's actual experience of the Christian church. In the past years Christians in the United States have expressed much interest in what are called base Christian communities. Base Christian communities, especially in Latin America, are groups that link faith and social action. Movements like marriage encounter, *Movimiento Familiar Cristiano,* charismatic renewal,

Jesus Caritas, Family Encounter, and Cursillo all emphasize the small-community structure. What they lack that base Christian communities have is political vision. The base Christian communities are not only culturally but also politically "radical," because they intend to work directly to challenge and change down to its very roots (hence, "radical") the social order in which we live.[5]

This way of linking faith and social action is a largely unknown phenomenon in an area where many think that religion only has to do with the "spiritual aspects of life," and that this approach, therefore, is an ineffective way to start a new mission. The Roman Catholic team that attempted a similar approach in south Texas did not achieve positive results. On the other hand, small prayer groups function relatively effectively, in part because they do not attempt to unite faith with social action, and focus instead on more personal problems such as illness, death, fears, and so forth.

The difficulty of trying to start base Christian communities should not be surprising. In Latin America they are the fruit of a long historical process, a process that is quite different from that affecting many of our members. While our members are among the poorest of the poor in this country, many of them are indeed upwardly mobile and have many of their basic needs met through government aid programs, thus taking away the much harsher sides of poverty that one sees in Latin America and which lead to social action there.

3. *Liturgical Style*

A highly emotional Pentecostal church service is very different from a traditional Roman Catholic Mass. To start with people's experience means that we will want to incorporate some aspects of both. We recognize that a Roman style may better fit with social stability and staying with the "mother church" as opposed to conversion and joining a new group. Since we are interested in starting new missions and in being sacramentally present in new places, we will want to be less structured in our services. We can be more emotional and spirited: we can say "Amen" when we agree with the preacher, "Gloria a Dios" after a testimony of faith, and we can cry during the prayers. The content of our preaching needs to emphasize conversion and to be very emotional.

4. Lay Leadership and Participation

Starting with people's experience also means using lay leaders for what was previously considered to be the work of ordained and seminary-educated clergy. A pastor with only 6 or 7 years of formal education who lives with the people and shares their cultural background and worldview is more effective than another who has 4 years of seminary tacked on to 16 years of formal education. Our lay pastor or evangelist will be more apt to interpret the Bible in terms the people understand. Another way of approaching this is to question what in fact comprises religious authority and leadership. In middle-class situations religious authority comes in part from reasoning clearly about the Christian faith, by presenting a sermon in a well-organized way that meets the questions and intellectual needs of the congregation. We often downplay and distrust emotion. Among our members, by contrast, an emotionally delivered testimony will have more authority than a well-organized but impersonal reflection upon one's faith.

While a low-key pastoral style involving good listening skills may be important in a middle-class setting, an authoritative and decisive approach to problems is often expected from our people.

Finally, pastors or trained lay evangelists cannot do all the work alone. Most other denominations that are growing in this area are using many people in their evangelization. When a new church building is opened a large number of lay people are there to attend services and develop social ties with new converts. Groups use evangelism teams that are well-equipped with musicians, films, and dynamic speakers. When we have more of a commitment on the part of *all* of our people to the evangelistic effort, and when our services are exciting, we also will grow.

10

BIBLE AND MISSION IN THE RURAL CONGREGATION

Virgil Thompson

Any significant discussion of Bible and mission in the rural Lutheran congregation must be cognizant of and address itself to three crises: the crisis of authority, the crisis of identity, and the crisis of community. The rural congregations of the church by no means have the market cornered on these three problems. They are issues which transcend both geographic and denominational distinctions within the church. Methodists, Presbyterians, and Roman Catholics, as well as Lutherans, face them. Christians who congregate in the cities and small towns of America, as well as those who congregate in rural America, face them.

My concern is to consider the topic of Bible and mission in the context of the congregational life of rural Lutherans. Although what I have to say here may have broader application, the specific purview of the essay focuses upon the questions of authority, identity, and community in the setting of rural Lutheran congregational life. My hope, of course, is that those who live and serve in such a setting will find the argument sufficiently engaging to enter into conversation with it. If in that way the praxis of rural ministry is advanced, then the purpose of the essay will have been served.

At the same time the essay invites those who live and labor in other corners of the vineyard (Roman Catholic inner-city parishes, Lutheran small-town parishes, Presbyterian suburban parishes) to read on, with the purpose of understanding better the situation and ministry of their brothers and sisters in Christ who live in the country. It may also be presumed, as this essay does, that there are sufficient similarities between what the church does out in the countryside and in the towns and cities so as to believe that Christians from the country and Christians from the city will have some common ground on which they might enter into fruitful conversation about Bible and mission. The topic, then, is ministry in a rural setting, but the conversation is not limited to those who reside there.

The argument of the essay takes up in turn: the fleshing out of the three issues which lie at the heart of the consideration of Bible and mission in a rural congregation; the reasons why these issues are characterized in terms of crisis; the foundation of a Lutheran response; and a constructive statement regarding how these issues might actually be addressed.

I

There can be scarcely any debate about the fact that the question of authority troubles the church in just about every phase of its life. One need not search very far to find evidence which illustrates the problem. Among Roman Catholics, papal authority is publicly challenged by theologians, priests, religious, and laity alike. The Vatican seems intent upon meeting the challenge with the sort of authoritarian ultimatums that remind Protestants of days gone by. Lutheran bishops in the midst of congregational strife and confusion—over such matters as conflict between the laity and the clergy, the relationship between religion and politics, gifts of the Spirit, social ministry, as well as problems unique to individual congregations—lament that they would like to do something but have no constitutional authority to intervene.

The problem is faced as well more directly in one's own pastoral service to the congregation. I recall vividly that in my first week of pastoral service a member of the congregation greeted me with the unsettling declaration: "Thompson, I want you to know that you are not my pastor. You may become my pastor but don't expect that there'll be anything automatic about it. Just because your name is on the office door does not mean that you'll have any actual commerce with us as pastor." Then and there I had the first suspicion that the pastoral office in that parish, at least, suffered a crisis of authority.

Over the years of pastoral service to the church the suspicion has not abated. Throughout the church symptoms of the crisis abound. In addition to the aforementioned examples one might cite the following as being symptomatic of the crisis: the sermon is held to be the mere opinion of the pastor. Congregations of the church flounder aimlessly, vulnerable to every sweet-talker who comes along. There seem to exist no universally recognized criteria by which conflict may be resolved, pastors and congregations disciplined, direction established, congregational policy formulated. Too often ecclesiastical conflict remains unresolved or ends in civil court. And too often ecclesiastical leaders resort to worn-out, cast-aside secular techniques for ordering the life of the church, management by objective, for instance.

The church in rural America, in addition to suffering these manifestations of the crisis, also experiences the crisis of authority in terms of the church's response to the faltering agricultural economy, which threatens the stability, vitality, and in fact the very survival of the family farm and the rural community. The troubles of the rural economy, with all the attendant ramifications for the people who live in rural America, have been addressed in church periodicals, seminars, and forums.

There is clearly a desire on the part of its devoted members that the church address itself to the plight of the rural community. But what is to be said? And by what authority? Is the church authorized to propose public policy regarding the rural economy? In what sense do the church's declarations regarding the rural economy differ from those of the Republicans or Democrats, or from those of the Farm Bureau or the Farmers' Union? Has the church a word from the Lord on this subject? May the church, for example, speak about the farm economy with the same authority with which it speaks of the forgiveness of sins? Regarding such questions no clear consensus exists among members of rural congregations.

One could go on mustering the evidence to substantiate the case, but perhaps enough has been said. The church currently suffers a crisis of authority.

The second crisis of which we have spoken, the crisis of identity, is closely related to the first. It is not just that familiarity with the Bible story of faith is woefully lacking among Christians (to the point of functional biblical illiteracy); not just that the confessional symbols seem a secret, rather well kept from the laity of the church; not just that they do not know their historic brothers and sisters who comprise the great cloud of witness which has gone before; not just that the children of the parish are hard pressed to determine precisely what distinguishes the adult community of the church from any other community. No, the congregations themselves find it difficult to articulate just what it is that distinguishes them as church. We seem to operate like a corporate amnesiac, uncertain where we have come from, who we are, and where we are going. The biblical witness and the historic confession of the church's faith all too often have not been given the voice which they demand and deserve in shaping the identity of the congregation. As a consequence the congregation suffers a crisis of identity with regard to what it means to be the one thing it is called to be—witness and servant of the gospel.

In responding to the crisis of identity, the church must of course seek to formulate its self-understanding on the basis of the historic faith. But it is not sufficient merely to repeat the old biblical and confessional formulas. Rather, the old formulas must be translated into the circumstances of contemporary life. In terms of the particularities of rural life, to which we have already made reference, Lutherans ask what difference their religious identity makes and does not make to the way in which they think and live. Does, for example, our Lutheran identity and heritage provide resources for dealing with adversity, personal stress, individual value, and other related human traumas which rural people face in this time? In order to answer these sorts of questions Lutherans must have a deeper familiarity with their distinctive traditions than is currently the case.

The third crisis which congregations of the church face is that of community. Those gathered on Sunday morning seem to have about as much in common as cars lined up at a gas station of their choice. We gather to get our fill of spiritual petrol. We then take our leave, perhaps having paused for a few moments of conviviality over coffee, without ever actually connecting with one another in any significant way. We seem a family estranged. The life of the community resembles Humpty Dumpty after the big fall. It has been assailed and fractured by the slings and arrows of political, economic, religious, family, and social strife.

We have heard the declaration that we are one in Christ. And yet, in responding to the problems which beset rural America, party association, denominational affiliation, political and social philosophy seem far more determinative. So often these sorts of differences seem to have a stronger pull on us than our solidarity in Christ. As a consequence, the isolation and loneliness of individual congregational members is absolutely overwhelming. Congregations of the church suffer isolation from one another as well. Lutherans seem unsure about their relationship to other Christians. We seem to have lost the sense of ourselves as a reforming movement in the church catholic. It is all regularly lamented, but we seem unable to heal it, making the community whole with acceptance and genuine care, whole in the solidarity of belonging and loving service of the gospel.

It is not a very cheering picture of congregational life in rural America. Some would no doubt argue that it really is not as bad as the picture has here been painted. This point may have some validity. Yet the fact remains that we suffer deep disparity between the promise regarding our life together and the actual state of affairs in our common life. If our assessment of rural parish life seems weighted toward the negative it is because we react against the usual slick, superficial, and overly rosy picture that has too often gotten all the press. Too, it is because we groan under the weight of this broken life for the redemption that is promised. We seek to be candid about that which is broken so that we might enter into the actual hurts of the congregation with the healing power of the gospel. No one has promised that congregational life would be a cruise on a love boat. We have no such expectations. We seek merely to be and to live as the church of Jesus Christ.

What then shall we say to this? What shall we say to it even if it is only the half of it, only the underside of congregational life in the countryside? It is this aspect of things, after all, which cries out for our attention. If the gospel has nothing to say to the brokenness of congregational life, it has very little to say that matters.

II

By way of response we begin with some very fundamental observations about the place of the Bible in the church and about the nature of the church's mission.

In his Lyman Beecher lectures, first published in 1907, Peter Taylor Forsyth argued that among the chief concerns of the church ought to be the restoration of "an intelligent and affectionate use of the Bible"[1] to the people of the congregations of the church. What Forsyth had in mind when he spoke of restoring to the people of the church an intelligent and affectionate use of the Bible is clarified when he reminds his readers "that Christ did not come to bring a Bible but to bring a Gospel." "The Bible," he continues, "arose afterwards from the Gospel to serve the Gospel. We do not treat the Bible aright, we do not treat it with the respect it asks for itself, when we treat it as a theologian, but only when we treat it as an apostle, as a preacher, as the preacher in the perpetual pulpit of the church. The charge of Jesus Christ," he concludes, "is to educate those people not in a correct theology, old or new, but in a mighty Gospel!"[2]

This is not to say that correct theology has no place in the life and ministry of the church; it certainly does have its place. Recognition must be given to the fact that the gospel is not about anything and everything. The gospel is a particular word. It is the good news of Jesus Christ, witnessed by the Scriptures and the confession of the church. The apostle Paul put it this way: "Since all have sinned and fall short of the glory of God, they are justified by his grace as a gift, through the redemption which is in Christ Jesus" (Rom. 3:23-24). That, according to the apostle, is the good news. It is the unconditional promise of God's free redemption. On the basis of that Pauline summary of the gospel, the reformers of the 16th century set forth their understanding of the gospel in the Article 4 of the Augsburg Confession: "It is also taught among us that we cannot obtain forgiveness of sin and righteousness before God by our own merits, works, or satisfactions, but that we receive forgiveness of sin and become righteous before God by grace, for Christ's sake, through faith."[3]

Theology is nothing but the labor of the contemporary church to identify that particular word which has been spoken by the apostles and confessors as gospel and to inform and shape its proclamation by that word. Theology, as one theologian has said, is what goes on in the mind of the church between the hearing and speaking of the gospel. It is the thought which the church gives to the task of speaking as gospel what it has heard as gospel from the witness of those who have gone before.

Correct theology, then, along with every other aspect of congregational life—preaching, administration of the sacraments, continuing Christian education, pastoral care, fellowship, service, and worship—are not ends in themselves. They all exist for the purpose of expanding the believing community and nurturing it in the gospel of Jesus Christ. That is the one end toward which all that we are and do as the church of Jesus Christ is directed. That is the mission ever before us. Though three-quarters of a century has elapsed since Forsyth issued his challenge, it has lost nothing of its urgency. Each generation of the church is confronted by the great commission of its Lord, "Go therefore and make disciples of all nations, baptizing them in the name of the Father and of the Son and of the Holy Spirit, teaching them to observe all that I have commanded you" (Matt. 28:19-20). To restore to the people of the church an intelligent and affectionate use of the Bible is then simply a matter of restoring them to the one mission for which they exist as church. It is making known in the community of faith the one gospel which animates, informs, and shapes its life as church.

This view of the relationship between the gospel—witnessed by the law, the prophets, and the apostles—on the one hand, and the mission of the church, on the other, Martin Luther never tired of underscoring. In the Smalcald Articles, for instance, he writes, "Thank God, a seven-year-old child knows what the church is, namely, holy believers and sheep who hear the voice of their Shepherd (John 10:3). So children pray, 'I believe in one holy Christian church.' Its holiness does not consist of surplices, tonsures, albs, or other ceremonies of theirs which they have invented over and above the Holy Scriptures, but it consists of the Word of God and true faith."[4]

The relationship between the Word of God as witnessed by the Bible and the mission of the church is further elaborated by Luther in the Small Catechism. There he makes clear the priority of the Word of God in the life and mission of the church: "I believe that by my own reason or strength I cannot believe in Jesus Christ, my Lord, or come to him. But the Holy Spirit has called me through the Gospel, enlightened me with his gifts, and sanctified and preserved me in true faith, just as he calls, gathers, enlightens, and sanctifies the whole Christian church on earth and preserves it in union with Jesus Christ in the one true faith. In this Christian church he daily and abundantly forgives all my sins, and the sins of all believers, and on the last day he will raise me and all the dead and will grant eternal life to me and to all who believe in Christ."[5]

Such a view of the relationship between the gospel and the mission of the church does not, however, originate with Luther and the confession of the Lutheran church. In the view of the 16th-century reformers, as well as in the view of those of us who continue to express our faith by those confessional symbols, the Bible itself insists upon this understanding of the relationship between the Word of God and the church. It is the Word of God alone which creates and sustains the life of the church in the direction of its God-given mission.

Regarding this point the Bible gives emphatic and absolute stress. The power of the Christian life and of the church in mission to the world does not lie in the Christian nor in the church. It lies in the Spirit of God, who works through the Word of God to create and sustain a people in the service of God. It simply is not the case, as so many seem to suggest, that God is resigned to standing around in the wings with hands in pockets, awaiting the decision of humanity to believe in the gospel and apply it in life. That view of the matter, as popular as it may be today, has nothing whatsoever to do with the biblical view. The Bible, as Lutherans insist, has quite a different view. According to the Bible it is not the case that believers must bring to life the Word of God. Rather, it is the case that the Word of God must bring believers to life and establish them in the purpose of God. As Paul has put it, "While we were yet helpless, at the right time Christ died for the ungodly. . . . God shows his love for us in that while we were yet sinners Christ died for us. . . . We know that our old self was crucified with him so that the sinful body might be destroyed, and we might no longer be enslaved to sin. . . . If we have died with Christ, we believe that we shall also live with him. . . . The death he died he died to sin, once for all, but the life he lives he lives to God. So you also must consider yourselves dead to sin and alive to God in Christ Jesus."[6]

Not only is the Word of God the power which initially creates and establishes the church. But the Word, where it is proclaimed in its purity, serves to sustain and reform the life of the church in keeping with its God-given mission. Nils Dahl argues that the early Christian cultus and the literature of the New Testament itself arose, at least in part, in response to the need for reminding the believing community of the privilege and the responsibility given to it through Baptism and incorporation into the church of Christ.[7]

Paul's exhortation to the Thessalonians is illustrative of this fundamental New Testament motif. In 1 Thess. 4:1-3 he admonishes: "Finally, brethren, we beseech and exhort you in the Lord Jesus, that as you learned from us how you ought to live and please God, just as you are doing, you do so more and more. For you know what instructions we gave you through the Lord Jesus. For this is the will of God, your sanctification. . . ." At this point in the letter the apostle goes on to relate specific instructions which were apparently especially pertinent to the Thessalonican situation. The point that Paul is laboring to make, as Dahl points out, is that "the initial acceptance of the gospel puts the whole of life under obligation. A community of baptized Christians which has come to share in the gospel and which has received basic catechetical instruction already knows what must be done. They have received the Holy Spirit and are on the right road. They need to preserve what they have received and to remind themselves of it in order to live out the reality into which they have been introduced. The first obligation of the apostle vis-à-vis a community is to make the faithful remember what they have received and already know—or should know."[8]

In other words, Paul contends that the church, like individual believers, lives in continual conflict between sin and righteousness, between faith and unfaith, between the bondage to Satan and the freedom in Christ. Thus the church must be constantly recreated and sustained by the Word of God.

It was this Pauline conviction, this motif of the apostolic witness, which animated the reformers of the 16th century. In the course of the Saxon parish visitations of 1528 Luther witnessed what becomes of the church when the lambs of Christ are not fed the Word of God. Following that visitation Luther could only conclude that the flock of Christ was being starved to death. To his friend Spalatin he wrote: "Conditions in the congregations are pitiable, inasmuch as the peasants learn nothing, know nothing, never pray, do nothing but abuse their liberty, make no confession, receive no communion, as if they had been altogether emancipated from religion."[9] Luther's response to this dismal state of affairs was to write the Small Catechism.

Conditions in the congregations of the church today need not be as desperate as they apparently were in the 16th century before we take up the concern for the reformation of the church and the education of the people by and in the mighty gospel of Jesus Christ. Yet the needed reformation, the ministry of building up the church in the gospel of Christ, will come only through faithful worship, serious and ongoing education, the responsible and compassionate care of souls, preaching that makes known the Word which promises salvation to the ungodly.

This is it. The mission of the church rises and falls on this one matter: Do our words—the public proclamation and the private witness—along with our actions—from our manner of institutional organization to our individual treatment of others—herald the good news that in Jesus Christ God has graciously acted to save the ungodly? It can never be a matter of whether we dare risk it. We can but pray that we ourselves, along with all preachers of the church and all who bear the name Christian, be brought to the point of passionate, single-minded devotion to Christ, to that point at which the apostle Paul's life found its direction and purpose: "Necessity is laid upon me," he said. "Woe to me if I do not preach the gospel!" (1 Cor. 9:16).

We can but pray, and take our stand in the tradition of Paul, Augustine, and Luther. Proclaim the one Word that matters, as if it were indeed the one Word that matters. One can seek, with all the courage and faith and wisdom and eloquence and stamina which can be mustered, to speak for and to this generation the good news that in Jesus Christ God has, unilaterally, of God's own gracious and sovereign will, acted to save the ungodly. There is no other place for us to stand and remain in the pulpit of the church. We have no other meaningful word to speak.

The gospel which the church has been given to live and to speak to the world does not answer all human questions, nor does it resolve all our earthly difficulties. As M. le Curé de Torcey of George Bernanos' *Diary of a Country Priest* has said,

> If only they'd let us have our way, the church might have given men that supreme comfort [of knowing that they are by God's own sovereign decision children of the heavenly Father]. Of course, they'd each have had their own worries to grapple with, just the same. Hunger, thirst, poverty, jealousy—we'd never be able to pocket the devil once and for

all, you may be sure. But man would have known he was the son of God; and therein lies your miracle.[10]

No, the gospel does not provide a blueprint for saving the family farm, nor an economic system that is fair and equitable for all, nor a politics that is a reflection of the kingdom to come. The gospel, however, is a word that will save us from our flights of utopian fancy, from our God-pretending, from the tendency of forever curving in upon ourselves. It will liberate us from the bondage to sin, death, and the devil. It will restore us to life in faith, hope, and love. It proclaims in advance God's final judgment of us. It tells us that God has a mind to count even the ungodly of God's own children. And one day God will complete what was begun in Jesus Christ, God's mission of redeeming the world.

Thus we hear the promise of God and we wait, groaning with all creation for the new day that is in the hand of God. We wait, and we work. Free. Down to earth. We work at the work which God has given us, for the well-being of others and the good of creation, to establish peace and justice. We go with no illusions about the continuing reality of sin, death, and the power of the devil. As the old priest in Bernanos' story had said, "We'll never be able to pocket the devil once and for all, you may be sure." Evil pervades the life of this world. It is out there: war, injustice, hunger, suffering, death, grief. The ways in which it manifests itself are legion. And it is not only out there; it is also in here, in the very heart of humanity. As we confess every Sunday, "We are in bondage to sin and cannot free ourselves. We have sinned against you in thought, word, and deed, by what we have done and by what we have left undone. We have not loved you with our whole heart; we have not loved our neighbors as ourselves."[11] We know better. That is not the problem. Rather, it is with us more a case of Paul's lament: "I do not understand my own actions. . . . For I do not do the good I want, but the evil I do not want is what I do. . . . Wretched man that I am! Who will deliver me from this body of death?" (Rom. 7:15a,19,24).

That is the anguished cry of humanity which the gospel answers. The gospel is the promise that Christ delivers us from sin, death, and the power of the devil. The church cannot manipulate nor manage nor harness that promise to serve some predetermined purpose. The church can but keep at the labor of getting it proclaimed in its purity and power. Then we wait for the Word to bring forth the fruits of the new creation.

It does happen. The Word goes forth to create a people alive in faith, hope, and love, a people free to live on this earth, working and waiting. And one day what God has begun in Jesus Christ and continues through the church in his name will come to full fruition. In the meantime we wait, remember, proclaim, and live accordingly, in a down-to-earth way, free of utopian dreams, free in faith and hope and love, free for the service which is of some earthly value.

III

Just so the foundation is laid from which we may address the threefold crisis which currently troubles the rural church.

With regard to the crisis of authority in the church, the problem comes down to the matter of being able to say what the gospel actually is and what it is not. The crisis of authority in the church is simultaneously a crisis of the gospel. The absence of authority in the church occurs only when the gospel has ceased to be spoken and heard. By the same token, authority is contingent upon the capacity and the boldness to speak the Word of God as it has been revealed in Jesus Christ.

Robert Jenson suggests that there are two aspects to authentic gospel speech. Our speaking of the gospel becomes authoritative in the community of faith when it is faithful to the remembered history (Bible and confession) and when, in response to the risen Lord, it functions in the lives of hearers as promise rather than law.[12] Such an understanding of authority in the church puts the matter in an entirely new light. In this light one is given to see that the problem of authority rests squarely upon the shoulders of those who are entrusted with the care of the congregation. If they do not know what the gospel is—if they are unfamiliar with what has been spoken by the apostles and confessors as gospel, if they lack the capacity to think through what has been heard to the end of speaking it in the new ways required by the new situation—then of course the gospel will not be spoken. The church will continue to suffer the crisis of authority. It will be of no avail to impose worldly models of authority. It will do no good to seek recourse to civil authority. Such solutions are woefully inadequate and will not answer the problem of authority in the church.

The crisis will only be resolved when those entrusted with the care of congregations recognize that before authority comes from below (from the community) it comes from above (from the Lord himself). Jesus Christ has himself authorized disciples (bishops, teachers, pastors, and leaders) to speak for him.[13] When they so speak his Word (which means, rather than merely repeating it, to speak it so that it does for the freedom of contemporary hearers what it did for past hearers) it will liberate the community from sin, death, and the power of the devil. Like sheep who know and heed the voice of the shepherd the people of the church will respect the authority of that voice which speaks the gospel. Without such contemporary, authoritative speaking of the gospel there simply will be no mission—in fact, no church. That makes of the absence of authority a crisis. One cannot overemphasize the urgency of the hour with regard to the question of authority in the church. We can no longer stand around lamenting that we have no authority within the community. That complaint only reveals that we have ceased speaking the gospel. We must resolutely set ourselves to the ministry of hearing, thinking, and speaking that Word which God has authorized us to speak, in the confidence that the lambs will hear and heed the voice of the shepherd.

At this point we must remind ourselves of Paul Tillich's distinction between the conditional and unconditional in life. By this he intended, I think, to get at the same sort of thing Luther intended to point out when he spoke of the things above and the things below.

Regarding the conditional in life—political, economic, and social realities—the church has no particular word from the Lord. It is not to say that God is uninterested in these realities, only that he has chosen to govern them through another means than the church.

Regarding the unconditional—the relationship of God to the creation, the goal of history, the identity of the redeemer—God has authorized the church to speak decisively. God has, for instance, bestowed to the church the authority to bind and loose sins.

The church must respect the distinction between the conditional and unconditional. It must not, for example, speak the unconditional answers of God in response to conditional questions. But to say that the church has nothing authoritative to say regarding what might be done to fix the faltering rural economy does not mean that the church has nothing to say that is relevant to rural people. Rather, by declaring the unconditional promises of God and thus having given assurance that God is taking care of those things above (salvation) believers are freed to grapple with the things below (rural economy) in a fashion that promotes the care of the earth and the well-being of others.

What I am saying is that the church has a particular word to speak, authorized by God—for instance, about sin. That word is called forgiveness. The church, however, has no particular word about the farm economy. About this matter Christians are encouraged to use reason and good sense to propose solutions which seem best to them, given what they know about God's intention for the creation. The answer to the question of the church's identity crisis is directly dependent upon the capacity of the church to speak authoritatively the gospel in and to the assembly of believers. The gospel by its very nature asserts a claim over those who hear. It announces that the gospel's promise of liberation from the bondage to sin, death, and the power of the devil for the freedom in Christ, the freedom to live as children of God is "for you." That new identity bestowed through the church's ministry of word and sacrament either becomes the chief element in one's self-definition or it has nothing whatsoever to say to a person. When and where the gospel is proclaimed with power and in its purity the question of one's identity is resolved. The gospel announces God's sovereign, unilateral decision: "You belong to me as my own child. You are destined for life that is fitting to that identity. No ifs, ands, or buts about it. "I, the Lord your God, have spoken."

At every turn in the life of the church that declaration must be made, that claim asserted over the life of community and individual believers. Belonging to the church is by Baptism and the claim there made. Living as church is by the Word and the Supper and the identity given there. All other aspects of a Christian's identity—vocation; political affiliation; social, economic, and family status; or whatever—is subordinated to the one identity of faith. No other consideration is permitted to overrule the claim of belonging and living as a child of God. Living out that identity is nothing, then, but being restored to the mission of getting it said in word and deed, the good news of God's gracious salvation.

We may suggest a similar response to our final consideration, the crisis of community. What unites individual believers as church is the gospel of Jesus Christ. That is the one Word by which the people of God cohere as church. It unites Christians in the solidarity of love (John 17:20-26). I could never hope to put it more powerfully than Paul Scherer has already said it:

> The Word that comes to [us] in that fellowship [of the church] comes to [us] there as in no other place. It comes to [us] in the mutuality of forgiving and serving love, battering down the walls of [our] loneliness, shattering the terror of [our] isolation. And it comes to create what it says. . . . It establishes a direction of its own. It probes far and deep toward the bedrock of human life. . . . There is no "by your leave" or "if you please" about it. It lays hold on everything and appropriates what it will. It leaves nothing unchanged. It fashions and transforms.[14]

The Word of God unites the people of God in a way that they could not and would not unite themselves. It sets them off in a direction that is not of their own choosing. By and in the power of God's Word the community is united in the mission of making known, through word and deed, the good news of God's gracious redemption. Along the way of that mission the church will not rest, just as its Lord does not rest, until all have been gathered in faith to proclaim, "Salvation belongs to our God who sits upon the throne, and to the Lamb!" (Rev. 7:10).

Lutherans have their place in the church catholic as a reforming movement which seeks to make this understanding of Bible and mission, the dogma of justification, central to everything in the life and theology of the church. The Lutheran community can never be content to live for itself. It exists to press the case for the absolute centrality of this view of the biblical message and its implied understanding of the church's mission to all that we are and do as church. It must ever seek to engage the entire Christian family precisely over this point, namely, that what animates, empowers, informs, and shapes the church as church is the good news, "the power of God for salvation to every one who has faith. . . . For in it the righteousness of God is revealed through faith for faith; as it is written, 'He who through faith is righteous shall live.' "[15]

11

A BIBLICAL PERSPECTIVE IN A MULTICULTURAL SETTING

Luis Alberto Pereyra

This essay will deal with some problems that we parish and inner-city pastors have to cope with daily in our continuing mission. Our field is a multicultural community where we want to serve and make visible the Bible as a means of God's revelation to those who are also included in his mission.

The Bible and Immigration

In Argentina, my mother country, I met families that came from Brazil. In earlier immigrations they had come from Germany following the First World War. They told stories about their cultural heritage which touched my heart. I remember that one family lived for a while without a home in the middle of the Brazilian jungle. They worked in the jungle cutting trees and selling wood. The whole family worked very hard, 15 hours a day, men, women, and children, old and young alike. After a long day they would gather around a campfire to eat and to read their Bible. One man told me that because they had lived for such a long time in the jungle he had learned to read German from his father's Bible and that he only knew how to read Gothic German. The Bible was the inspirational book and the school text of this family. Their father was both teacher and pastor to them. I had the privilege to hold in my hands that old and historical Bible. They showed it to me as their most precious treasure.

Ten years ago I started to work in a Norwegian-American congregation in Brooklyn, and I confess that it was very difficult for me to understand their cultural heritage. The Norwegian immigrants not only brought their culture with them but their faith as well. Bay Ridge was one of the areas of this cultural implantation, and after a century there is still evidence of a Scandinavian presence.

Immigration placed a tremendous evangelistic responsibility on the Norwegian-Americans in this society. Sunday school was a field for evangelism, and for acculturation as well. In the 1890 Annual Report of Trinity Lutheran Church we read: "The Sunday School has worked steadily and fruitfully this past year for the purpose of implanting the Evangelical Lutheran Confessions in Scandinavian children in South Brooklyn."[1] This statement shows clearly the care and concern for those from Scandinavian countries. We note that in its mission Trinity congregation was faithful not only in the ministry of Word and Sacrament, but also in meeting the material needs of poor Scandinavians.[2] The Lutheran Medical Center in our community is still a living testimony of their faith and love.

In October 1975, Trinity received a new challenge to its life and history. Trinity decided to open its doors for a Hispanic ministry. Its whole life has been affected by that decision.

Exile and Diaspora for Our Immigrants

The presence of the Hispanic culture in a Norwegian-American setting brings us another step. This we may understand in the light of the biblical record as analogous to the experience of the people of Israel when they had to cope with exile.

By the end of the 19th century the Norwegian immigration had slowed, because of economic reasons. In the middle of the 20th century there was a massive immigration to this country from Puerto Rico, also for economic reasons. Two decades later, this immigration was expanded by people from South and Central America who came here for both economic and political reasons. In 587 B.C. Nebuchadnezzar had put an end to the national existence of Jerusalem and then to the kingdom of Judah.[3] Whether Jews or Norwegians or Hispanics, those who had to be in the Diaspora in a new country in a new and very different society faced a very painful situation. What do these experiences of exile and immigration have to tell us? We are directed to those biblical foundations which can help us to resolve our contemporary problems and look for the ways in which the Word of God can lead us as God's own people.

The political, social, and religious life of Israel changed radically. The people were dispersed throughout the empire where they began to form small colonies for the purpose of mutual support and education. The religion of the Jewish people altered as well. Babylonian customs made an impact on those from Judah, who were called to account because of their involvement in pagan worship.[4] This was the time of writing of the Servant Songs of Deutero-Isaiah, who sets forth the meaning of their relationship with God and their own history. Frequently we find a strong emphasis on creation (Isa. 43:1; 45:18). There was a continuing conflict between faith in Yahweh and Babylonian idols and myths as these affected their worship life (Isa. 42:17; 44:1-18; 45:22). The real problem was the impact upon the religious values of the Israelites of the values of their oppressor. Psalm 137 expresses how difficult it was for the Israelites to share their personal and national faith with those who had subjected them to slavery and exploitation. In spite of their wrongdoing, these exiles held to Judah as their spiritual homeland and Jerusalem their holy city.[5]

The prophets articulated the great themes of justice, the return to their land, and God as Savior and Liberator. The theme of liberation had an eschatological dimension, and arose out of the suffering of the people and their dreams for the future (Isa. 45:8; 47:4). To participate in pagan worship, therefore, was to be integrated into the life-style and culture of those who oppressed the Israelites (Ezekiel 14) and denied that hope. Jeremiah and Ezekiel saw signs of life in the communities of the exile. Those small communities maintained their faith and their culture. They were also literary centers, places of theological reflection, where much of Old Testament theology was fashioned.

The New Testament also refers to groups of people who lived in other forms of dispersion. The Gospels and Epistles have particular concern for such groups, but the Word of God was addressed to them as the common faith of the first Christian communities. While the entire New Testament has concern for those who believe in Jesus Christ,

1 Peter, Hebrews, and Revelation should receive special attention. These are letters of consolation for those who suffered persecution for being Christians in the context of their own communities.

The introduction of 1 Peter is addressed to those who are described as "the exiles of the Dispersion. . . ." Its caring is addressed toward a variety of persons, such as free men and women (2:16), household slaves (2:18-20), wives with nonbelieving husbands (3:1-6), husbands with Christian wives (3:7), community leaders-elders (5:1-4), and recent converts (younger persons 5:5). The author is concerned also with "visiting strangers" (1:1; 2:11) and "resident aliens" (2:11; cf. 1:17). The society was a rainbow, a mixture of languages, rites, and customs.[6] There the church performed a truly liberating work. It was a melting pot where the cultural diversity of the members enriched their testimony as a community of faith in a time of dispersion. Everybody had different roots and traditions and this reflected the complexity of the Roman Empire. We can easily compare it with many communities in the United States, where our lives are also shaped by multicultural influences. For the author of this letter the church was inclusive and at the same time sensitive to those who needed pastoral caring (cf. 1 Peter 5).

Hebrews is a letter of doctrine that reinterprets Jewish concepts within a Christian framework. The final three chapters contain reflections on the faith in terms of living testimonies. The spiritual values of this community emerge not only from doctrine but also from lives of believers who have suffered for their faith. The author challenges his readers to share with each other the burden of the cross.

Revelation is a fascinating book, colorful, musical, and liturgical. It is full of hymns (4:8; 4:11; 5:9-10; 5:12-13; 7:1,12,15-17; 11:17-18; etc.). Those addressed were enduring persecution. Its message not only points to a future blessedness but is intended for those who are in the fire of daily struggle. This book of liturgy and songs was full of their life situations, and its climax was their liberation through Jesus, the Lamb of God. There is a parallel here with the Servant Songs of Deutero-Isaiah. Jerusalem is still pictured as the Holy City, but Palestine is no longer the spiritual homeland. It is this new reality that Christians were called to witness to before the world (14:12; 21:4-5).

The experiences of exile and dispersion of these early Christian communities are rich in material for counseling those in need. The writers fed not only their own communities; still today their work feeds the church. Together with those first believers, we can sing, beyond temporal boundaries, with the church in the New Testament and those in exile.

This is the background that we were looking for. There are tremendous multicultural expressions of the Christian faith in the Bible. What can the Bible teach us today about the future we must face in the city?

Who Are Our Newcomers?

If we want to understand the present situation we must go back in American history. From the days of the early Spanish conquerors much of this country was Hispanic territory. Almost the entire South was claimed by Spain. Hispanic immigration, therefore, started long before the beginning of this century. Hispanics, together with American Indians, were part of this country before any other Europeans arrived here. As a result of wars and treaties, Hispanics today are strangers and foreigners in what was their own land. The Hispanic community in the western hemisphere is made up of 600 million people, living from the Rio Grande to Tierra del Fuego, speaking one language and holding one faith.

The Hispanic people who immigrated to the United States have had to adapt themselves to an entirely different culture. They had to struggle initially with problems of housing, jobs, and education. Later they found themselves trapped in a system which subjected them to economic oppression.[7]

The Latin-American immigration was the first to enter this country unaccompanied by their native clergy. Immigrants from European and Scandinavian countries, on the other hand, came with their own teachers and priests or pastors. Religion was very important for those Hispanic "newcomers." Among the difficulties they had to face was a lack of priests and pastors.

Hispanics also confronted the problems of education and job opportunity. The following figures depict educational levels among Hispanics in the United States:[8]

Eighth grade or less	31%
High school, 1-3 years	30%
High school graduate	24%

Some college	12%
College	3%

Such low levels of education make it difficult for Hispanics to compete in the job market. The large number of job-training programs created for Hispanics proves the magnitude of the problem.

Another issue is the catechesis or Christian education of Hispanics. Those who want to join the Lutheran church or other traditional denominations must learn a white and transcendental Christology. Latin American liberation theologians begin by pointing out the schizophrenia in which people live, the gap between the God of beyond and the demands of real life, here and now.

The core of the problem is how we can face our reality with a Christology which is totally strange to our life-style, heritage and culture. The term *white Christology* is borrowed from black theology. James C. Cone, a contemporary black theologian, helps us understand the difference between white and black Christology.[9] In Cone's view, white Christology is a Christology of the oppressors because it leads to oppression where neither oppressors nor oppressed can be liberated.

Cone and Virgilio Elizonda[10] mount an attack against the system of education in the United States which, in their view, creates a class of people ready to be exploited. The oppressors have domesticated them, and made them subservient to those who believe that their God defines their lives and history.[11] Cone describes the tragedy of a people who had passed through a process of liberation but must go to white seminaries to receive theological education and there be domesticated under the shadow of the almighty and transcendent God. A biblical hermeneutic for Christian education focuses on poor and the oppressed, and encourages them to participate in the whole process of their liberation.[12]

Many churches, like Trinity Lutheran in Brooklyn, will have problems when they plan to undertake a "mission *for* the Hispanics," rather than "*with* the Hispanics." We are Christians; we, like Lutherans, were baptized "in the name of the Father, and of the Son, and of the Holy Spirit." We have, however, a different approach to the Bible as a living Word of God. It is as though God were still with us in our journey between Egypt and the Promised Land. As a part of our liturgy at Trinity, we pray every Sunday, and ask the people what they want to pray for. Their prayer requests are simple, but rooted in their daily lives.[13] The poor in our communities do not know all the fine points of theology and doctrine, or whether the Bible, as the Word of God, is "inerrant" or "infallible." They do believe Jesus' words in the gospel: "Go and tell John what you have seen and heard: the blind receive their sight, the lame walk, lepers are cleansed, and the deaf hear, the dead are raised up, the poor have good news preached to them" (Luke 7:22-23). The kingdom of God has invaded their lives. That is why we, contrary to some white churches, see that the gospel has implications for such issues as the independence of Puerto Rico, the invasion of Granada, the Malvinas War, El Salvador and Nicaragua, the political process in Argentina and Brazil, the Simpson Mazzoli bill, the sanctuary movement, unemployment, education and health, drug addiction, alcoholism, housing, the homeless, etc. Frequently we hear the response to this agenda, "Brother, we preach Christ crucified. Christ is the hope."

The Bible as a Source of Liberation

We have found fundamental theological and biblical resources for our mission today in a multicultural setting. Now we ask ourselves, how can three different cultures be together in mission? Mission to whom? What are the issues we have to deal with? What procedures should we follow? All these questions could be answered as we work together. What is needed, however, is a process of conversion, carried out in a liberating way.

St. Paul has written: "For we are contending against the principalities, against the powers, against the world rulers of the present darkness, against the spiritual hosts of wickedness in the heavenly places" (Eph. 6:12).

What are these "principalities" and "powers" and "world rulers"? For years many churches identified these realities with smoking, drinking alcoholic beverages, sexual behavior, etc. Sin was seen as an expression of individual failure that makes one feel guilty. Paul instead encourages us to discover the true nature of these "principalities," to see sin in its full human dimension. The next step is conversion to a new understanding of faith and consequent behavior. If we realize, for instance, that our congregation and community have a racist attitude which prevents people of color from equal participation, then the next step will be to announce that prophetic word which will lead them to a true commitment to the universal gospel (cf. Gal. 3:28). We do not realize how difficult it is for those who maintained such a negative attitude toward blacks, Hispanics, Asians, or other cultures to change, to repent, to turn to the way of the Lord. It may be easier to quit smoking than to love those whom we have hated for a lifetime.

How can the Bible help us with this problem, and how can we see the Word of God as a living hope for our communities? The Bible shows us that one of the ways that God addresses God's people is by calling them to conversion. The word that Isaiah and other prophets use for conversion is *šûb*. Isaiah is not talking precisely about an "altar call"; he is talking about a "change of attitude," a return to Yahweh. The prophet preaches about this attitude and his voice unmasks the false conscience, explains the sin, and identifies the wicked.[14] The word *šûb* is not used only in respect to religious concerns, like the worship of other gods. This opens a new understanding of the social and political concerns of the Bible. Amos 4:6-12, for example, does not deal with "other gods" but about the people who "did not return to me" (v. 9). In the context of this book, to "turn" to Yahweh is to practice socioeconomic justice and legal respect for the poor who claim their rights in the courts.[15] The tragedy occurs when the people do not want to hear. Then the Bible talks about those who "refuse" or become "rebels." We find the words *bēt merî*, "rebellious house" (Ezek. 2:3,6-8; 3:9,27), as a designation for the nation which refused to hear the prophetic voice. That "house" or "people" has, according to the prophet, a hard heart and they will not hear the voice of God. Ezekiel deals with this theme in 3:7f.; Jeremiah also talks about their "faces harder than rock" (5:3). The theme is also taken up by Mark and John in the New Testament in those passages where Jesus sees the warning of the prophet in his disciples' attitude (Mark 6:52; 8:17; John 12:40).

The call for a conversion of congregations which have racist, sexist, and class attitudes is constant (see the picture of Jesus in Rev. 3:20). The people of Israel were not ready to carry out the work of God until they repented. Our congregations as they are cannot be part of God's mission to the poor, the oppressed, and the homeless. They still want to perpetuate a white agenda as their top priority. The prophets also spoke about how senseless it is to have beautiful sanctuaries and liturgies if all of that is an expression of *incurvatus in se,* turning in upon oneself (Amos 5:21-24; Isa. 1:10-17). The Bible is clear about the mission to the poor and the oppressed.

Approaching a New Christology

One of the gifts that we receive from the Hispanic people is their reflection on what has come to be called liberation theology. We can come to a better understanding of our own situation with the help of their theological vision. Liberation theology brings to light a new dimension of Christ. Liberation theologians distinguish between pure reflective discourse—closer to the metaphysical and divorced from the reality—and praxis, which receives its focus "from" reality and therefore deals in a Christian context with poverty, dependence, and multiple forms of exploitation.[16]

White congregations and communities have often developed their theologies with the presupposition that their values are not only different but superior. Their hermeneutic in approaching reality is derived from the concept of a transcendent God who is absent from human history. God is viewed as Master (subject) of history and humanity God's object. Liberation theology, by way of contrast, considers humans both as creatures and as coworkers in God's creation.

In expressing the gospel in our own community, we would focus on education, welfare, housing, health care, salaries, unemployment, racism, sexism, classism, etc. These areas are mirrored in Jesus' agenda in Luke 4. Luke 4, of course, is not the whole gospel, but it is also the gospel. We affirm the sovereignty of God in all those areas where the poor and the oppressed are present. We do not see sin merely as moral failure but as possessing a demonic and cosmic dimension (Rom. 8:22-23) which is defeated by the death and resurrection of our Lord.

For many of our congregations it is easier to send money and pray for missions in Africa, Asia, or South America than to reach Hispanics, blacks, or Asians in their own communities. It is easier to send money and pray for seminarians in Africa than call a black as a senior pastor in a white congregation. For some it may be hard to listen to a sermon and receive the sacrament from a woman. We are not talking about opposition to one another; we are pointing out a crisis of values from a Christian viewpoint.

The multicultural reality can be a beautiful rainbow of people where the church of Christ is present in our communities. This is a field of continuing mission. It is mission where the Bible talks to the people as they are and brings hope to the multicultural setting, where Christ is seen alive, walking daily in the streets as God's own expression of love, hope, and salvation.

12

THE BIBLE AND THE NEW CONGREGATION: ONE PASTOR'S STORY

Debra Grant

Everyone has a Nineveh—that certain place which you are convinced is littered with all the refuse of society, or at best, many well-meaning but extremely confused people. It is that place which no seminarian dare speak too loudly either for or against lest the Most High actually hear and send him or her there. Growing up in New England, I was certain that the South was such a Nineveh for me.

Before entering the seminary, I answered God's call to ministry with a resounding "Maybe." I even went so far as to say, "Here I am, Lord, send me—see footnote: anywhere but the South." I realized at the time it was hazardous to make such a clause in the contract. I felt a certain kinship with Moses who upon receiving his call found it easier to whine and complain than to say an outright no to God.

I began to smell something "fishy" when I was assigned to the Southeastern District of the American Lutheran Church. Three months after graduation I waited for a call to a congregation in the unknown South. This period of time was as close as this Lutheran can get to purgatory. I received a call not from a congregation but from a division of the national church. The Division for Service and Mission in America wanted me to start a new congregation in Nashville, Tennessee. I thought I was doomed.

Though I was surrounded with some sympathetic voices which said, "Don't do it. . . .You can always say no. . . .Change districts," the smell of the inside of a whale belly began to grow stronger. I could say no to the DSMA but saying no to God's call to that place was far more difficult. (This is worth noting since there are often many who question whether the voice of the church and the voice of God are saying the same thing; once in a while, they actually do!)

I accepted the call, but not without a lot of whining and complaining. Who could hear it inside a whale belly anyway? Except maybe God and the whale and a few close friends who wanted to swap notes concerning whether their whale belly smelled the same as mine.

I am explaining how I got to Nashville because it shows how one's preconceptions can be challenged, and also because it gives a flavor of what to expect from this chapter. As the introduction implies, this pastor derives a great degree of comfort in finding biblical parallels to life-situations. Since most ministers involved in missions wonder if they are doing things "right," it is nice to know there is some biblical precedent for what we are about.

The other aspect that needs to be mentioned here is the personality of doing mission, a Lutheran mission, in the middle of the Bible Belt. I won't make generalizations about new congregations in other settings because this is the only setting I know and pretend to understand. For the most part, this is the chronicle of the whining and complaining of a fool for Christ.

Traditionally, Lutherans in the United States have put their best evangelical efforts into the nursery. In other words, the church has usually grown by birth. New congregations, therefore, usually began where there was an identifiable group of people who were born and cut their teeth on Luther's Small Catechism. Then someone had the bold notion that for the church to be active, growing, and vital, we needed to reach out to those whose tastes might not lean toward bratwurst and lutefisk. Consequently, the church began to plant new congregations in places which were simply growing with people who were not necessarily Lutheran and not even churched.

Goodlettsville, a northern suburb of Nashville, Tennessee, is such a place. With a population of 11,000—expected to double by 1990—it stands nervously at the edge of the country's southern migration. The conservative people want the revenue and benefits of a growing community but they are also vocally concerned about the changes they will bring.

Within the city limits of Goodlettsville there are 17 churches: one Presbyterian, two United Methodists, two Southern Methodists and a variety of flavors of Baptist; the majority of all the rest are Churches of Christ, a fundamentalist, New Testament-oriented group with a heavy law emphasis. The Churches of Christ began when some people decided that the Southern Baptists were getting too liberal. Few people who are natives to this area even know how to spell "Lutheran." Those who have heard believe us to be, at best, "like the Catholics," and at worst, "like a cult." Add to the strangeness of the Lutheran church in the South a female pastor from Massachusetts, and one has what some tactful people have termed "a challenge."

Being a stranger in a strange land it was most apparent that what I needed to do most was *listen.* Without a ready-made congregation to which to listen, I listened wherever there were people talking. I listened to the local news, caught snatches of conversations in grocery stores and waiting in lines. I talked with city officials and real estate agents. Learning the territory is that much more difficult without someone who already knows the ins and outs. I learned more by accepting my stupidity than by trying to fit in prematurely.

What I learned from my listenings is that the church is not simply a part of the community life here, it permeates the community mind-set. Everyone knows the language of the faith. People of every vocation, every age, every economic level know how to talk "church." Though the average church attendance here is not much higher than the national average, the people know the words and phrases of church life. Since they do, the ones who want little to do with the church can effectively fight off the hard-sell evangelists. The truly unchurched, therefore, are difficult to identify simply by listening to the God-talk.

One incident which occurred early after my arrival taught me about the mind-set of the people and the use of the language. It also taught me that I needed to improve my listening skills.

After having seen the ad for our new congregation in the newspaper, an elderly woman called me to ask some questions. I arranged to meet with her at her home. She gave me some family history and said that she had attended a Baptist church in town but had never joined. She was open to new ideas and asked me, "What do the Lutherans believe?"

In this setting, that question is more complicated than it sounds. There is the danger of sounding too different from the other churches, as we certainly are theologically and liturgically. People are suspicious of the differences. There is also a danger in looking nonsensical if we sound too much the same. After all, we do lift up the same God, tell the same story, and do not claim a corner on the gospel of Jesus Christ. How, then, do I answer this question with an attractive balance of both that is less than a paragraph or two long? My position papers in seminary, though a wonderful exercise, were of no use.

Fortunately, this woman helped me by asking a follow-up question, "What do Lutherans believe about Baptism?" How wonderful, I thought. Baptism is at the very core of Lutheran theology, worship, and church life! Certainly I could explain to her the similarities and differences of Christians who are Lutherans most eloquently through the explanation of Baptism. And so I did. At great length.

She very patiently took it all in. What she was doing with it I did not stop to find out. When I finally satisfied my need to tell her everything critical to Lutheran baptismal theology, I paused politely for questions. The woman screwed up her lovely face and after a thoughtful pause said, "I don't care about all that—d'ya sprinkle or dunk?"

From that time on I focused more attention on listening not only to the stories but understanding the questions. The questions were put in language that was familiar to me but meant something else entirely. The single issue of Baptism is filled with many different perspectives in this setting than the more theological, academic one I was familiar with. Baptism in the South is more like a Christian Bar Mitzvah—a rite of passage for a young teenager. It has little to do with God and much more to do with that person coming of age in the faith and being saved. The Lutheran practice of baptizing babies is met with as much disdain as snake handling.

Besides Baptism the other significant difference has to do with the perspectives on the Bible. How the Bible is treated has an effect on the kind of people who are attracted or not attracted to a Lutheran congregation in the South.

The best way to get at this view is to look at the three important steps for studying the Bible: (1) What does the Bible say? What do the literal words of the Scriptures say? (2) What does the Bible mean? This involves interpreting the words and phrases to get at the meaning of what was being said. (3) How do we apply it? How should we then live? The emphasis of the majority of the people rests on the first and third questions.

Scripture is memorized, quoted, and plucked out of context. It is used as an owner's manual, an encyclopedia of quick spiritual cures, or a book of quotations with pithy sayings for moral living. It is then applied as a model for godly living and, more often than not, a list of don'ts and don'ts (there are not too many clear dos in the Bible but plenty of don'ts).

That problematic middle question—"what does the Bible mean?"—is ignored. It is too difficult and it puts the Scriptures under too much human scrutiny. The middle question invites the use of historical-critical scholarship for the purpose of getting at the Word of God through understanding the meaning of the words of God.

The asking of the middle question has evoked three different reactions among those who are interested at all. The first is suspicion and disdain from those who embrace the first and last questions only and find no good reason for asking the middle one. According to them, the question of what the Bible means is answered simply by what it says. Any other view to the contrary and which looks too closely at the totality of Scripture is considered not to be of God. It follows then that they would view the Lutheran congregation as a representative of a liberal group which is sure to fail without God on their side. Members who are loyal and content in their local denominations have chosen to ignore the new congregation—"it will go away."

The other two reactions are represented by people who have shown an interest in our new congregation. The second reaction comes from those who at one time had been immersed in the conservative mindset but found that trying to make a magnum leap between biblical times and the present was an insult to their intelligence. They are people who have asked some important questions concerning how the Bible is applied, such as in the issues of school prayer, abortion, creationism, etc. These people are looking for more to God's story that will touch their own lives more deeply.

These same people have made comments which provide some valuable insights on their past church experience. These comments often go like this, "I feel so good after worship here. . . . I feel a little guilty, I didn't think church was supposed to feel good. . . ." Whether or not those feelings are an accurate representation of what other churches intend to convey is not the issue. People drop out of church for as many reasons as they drop back in.

The issue is for us to ask what can we offer to those who have dropped out because of a perspective on the words of God. Words which were picked out for them and only caused them to feel worse about themselves convicted these people so much of their inability to keep the law that they gave up trying. These are people who left the church because the gospel was not alive for them in anything they witnessed. Worship itself became a kind of penance which provided temporary relief from the guilt of angering a somber God.

I asked one new member how she would describe our theological perspective to another person from a conservative background. She said, "Realistic. You can sense it when you walk in the door; folks come dressed as they are. They are comfortable in whatever they want to wear, jeans and a T-shirt, or dresses, suits, and ties. Everybody's the same. And then right at the beginning of the service we admit in front of God and everybody that we are sinners. In the South, you're not supposed to be a sinner so you don't talk about it even if you are. Here we admit it right off the top, get forgiven, and we're free to listen, learn, and feel good about ourselves and God." A mission congregation which is based on the Word of God and which emphasizes both law and gospel as our church does has a tremendous potential for those familiar only with the condemning and convicting words of God.

The third reaction comes from those who are taking a second look at the church, not for spiritual, theological reasons, but for social reasons. These people have rejected or been rejected by the church because of the character of their life-style. This includes people who are simply looking for God to put a seal of approval on life-styles they have no intention of changing, to the divorced, to those who would like to enjoy a beer without wrestling with their conscience. They are people who for a variety of reasons don't feel as though they fit into a community and yet still need the support and fellowship of a community.

A church such as ours whose theology stresses grace and freedom and which is willing to dare to ask the question, "What does the Bible mean?" is attractive. It is an appealing perspective but one which can be easily abused by ignoring the responsibility of being a child of God.

Some of our people have no history with a clear understanding of the Word of God. They do have a history with the words of God which they have reduced to the words of people whose writings have no more credibility or authority than a gossipy national tabloid. Worship for them is a time for peace, collecting thoughts, and making some vague spiritual connection to a greater power.

Though such persons admire the church for its willingness to ask the question of what the Bible means, they have no intention of asking the question themselves. Bible study for them is a waste of time, but a good discussion group on a timely issue is helpful.

From these reactions, I have been able to determine a few implications for the ministry of this new congregation and how I approach the people as pastor. The first implication is in preaching. Any sermon which is conversational and not "preachy" in style and which does not run over 20 minutes receives rave reviews. Because of the negativity to Bible study, the preaching often takes on the teaching task simply to offer a well-balanced meal to those who only want to eat the stuff that tastes good.

This teaching/preaching approach also helps those who are seeking to hear the words of God and the Word of God which they failed to recognize or was not shown to them before. The bad press that the Bible has been assigned makes it that much more difficult to organize a Sunday school or adult Christian education. "I need friends; I don't need old stories that cramp my life-style." Opportunities for teaching, like opportunities for counseling, happen outside the classroom setting in parking lots, on front porches, while weeding the garden, etc. It is indeed a difficult responsibility to communicate the Word of God in the words of God when the words have been made a stumbling block for so many.

Besides combining the teaching and preaching tasks, another implication for ministry is in using different language for the old, old story. The language, however, cannot be so different that it supports the suspicion that the Lutheran church is a cult. The old words such as *salvation, redemption, sin, glory, reconciliation* and phrases like *born again, Jesus died for you* and *God is love* fall rather flat from overuse. Even these words have become separated from the depth of their meaning. It is difficult to speak seriously of the gospel when the words we use might be enshrined in refrigerator magnets holding up the grocery list.

The choice I am faced with, then, is to use the traditional words to stay as faithful to the words of God as possible or to use other words that are true to the Word of God as I understand it. Either way I take a risk. There is the cost of potentially misrepresenting the gospel or losing the interest of a person for the sake of scriptural purity. It is not a risk I take lightly. But I do take it. More often than not, I take the risk of using a different language for the sake of the one who might hear the gospel for the first time.

Without using the word *sin,* I can speak of self-centeredness and our desire to be God. Instead of *resurrection,* I can speak of Jesus getting up alive after being quite dead. Many times the language depends on whom I am talking to. After a few unsuccessful attempts, I was able to communicate Baptism to a semiilliterate construction worker by describing it as a good, solid foundation that was already laid for him as a headstart on his life. To a mother racked with guilt, unable to understand God's love for her, I suggested a connection between the tenacity of her love for her not-always-good daughter with the even greater tenacity of God's love for her.

As I imagine it is in any ministry setting, the language used and the methods of ministry depend largely on the quality of the listening that has been and continues to be done.

Besides the God-talk which permeates the language in the South, another thing which has biblical connections and is an obvious part of the landscape is the church buildings. When I first came to my "Nineveh" I did not have a church building or church members. The DSMA has a manual to describe the steps toward organization and a training event to teach about management and styles of ministry. I was still at a loss as to what I needed to do to go from nothing to a brick building with a steeple which is what everyone in the South expects you to do.

I asked the best expert available, a colleague who had begun a new congregation the year before. I asked him, "What do I do first?" He said, "What was the first thing the patriarchs did when they arrived in a new place?" "They built an altar." "Go and do likewise," he said.

The altar was a folding table from a local discount store covered with the least expensive white tablecloth I could find. The paraments were hand-me-downs from other congregations and the cross was a gift from my internship church. It was pretty outstanding, considering that the first altars were just a pile of rocks! We built the altar in a music studio we rented on Sunday mornings. We set aside for God a space and by doing so we made a room with cheap paneling and buckling linoleum floors a holy place.

The same colleague who set me in motion also wrote a song about mission congregations. One line says, "and now we meet in places you'd have to see to believe. . . ." Within my district there are congregations which have had their beginnings in a fire hall, a shoe store, a wing of a Baptist church, a country club, a bar, a bank, a movie theater, and a funeral home. The task of the present-day mission congregation is very much involved in turning the secular into the sacred.

I used to be quite annoyed with the members' necessity for a church building, especially expensive space which is used on a limited basis. It is, however, the story of the people of God in the wilderness that provides some comfort and understanding.

As long as we have been God's chosen people, we have been a people for whom a sense of place has been important. The altar set aside for God gives a visual reminder that God is in this place. The act of building an altar in the most mundane spaces enables us to claim a holy place for God and God's people. The building of the "first unit," as the DSMA calls it, has some important spiritual connections for a people who have known a kind of wilderness. In John's revelation of the kingdom of Heaven, such holy places will not have to exist because all will be holy. Until then, our holy spaces, wherever we can make them, are important parts of the church's life.

The role of the Bible in this new congregation can be seen in how it parallels some of the stories of Scripture: the story of Jonah, the wandering people of God, and the importance of holy places. We have also seen in the Bible Belt that our mission of God's Word is effected by the proliferation of God's words. All the while we are challenged to do as Jesus did—to listen, to learn, to love. The most awesome task before us as we attempt to establish a congregation in a place that is filled with the words of the gospel is *to be the gospel.* To make the good news new means not only to know the words of the Bible but to be the living Word of God in the midst of the people.

We are called as God's people not just to speak words of love but to love, to love without counting the cost, to love with mad abandon. The great paradox of Scripture is also seen in the irony of a new congregation. The emphasis of the first years is on survival, reaching toward being self-supporting, but a congregation cannot grow and become self-supporting without taking risks, without reaching out beyond itself, without being willing to do ministry in this place even if it means death. Therein lies the truth and the mystery of the work we are all about.

13

BIBLE AND MISSION IN A CENTER-CITY CONGREGATION

John F. Steinbruck

The center of the city—where its guts are generally located—is usually the intersection of "the good, the bad, and the ugly." It is a far cry from the shalom vision Walter Brueggemann declares:

> The central vision of world history in the Bible is that all creation is one, every creature is community with every other, living in harmony and security toward the joy and well-being of every other creature.[1]

All too often our urban species reveals the darker side of cruelty over compassion, competition over coexistence, choosing death over life until the city is more a curse than a blessing. Thus we minister in an environment of what is often a total contradiction to the Deuteronomic mandate paraphrased above.

Central Washington, D.C., is such a place, particularly Thomas Circle, where Luther Place Church is located, within sight of the White House a few blocks south. It is a parish that is a study of contrasts from the powerful to the powerless, the rich and the poor, the resident and transient, the healthy and the sick, straight world and underworld, the established and the homeless, old and young, black and white, high-rise, house dwellers and grate people. Looking south, one sees the federal facade associated with Washington, D.C.; north is the 14th-Street corridor of unemployment, drugs, residential areas still bearing the scars of the burning in the 1968 "uprising"; west are posh hotels, the Embassy of the USSR, beginning embassy row up Massachusetts Avenue, symbols of power and special interests from the Washington Post, the National Rifle Association, American Medical Association, National Education Association, National Geographic; east is the way of the wretched, where the sick and homeless are systemically driven downward and out of view of respectable Washington. All of this constitutes a mosaic of worlds and issues that run the gamut from president to prostitutes who gather daily in large numbers all about Luther Place. And slipping between the cracks of Washington's high-powered structures are the homeless nomads wandering the urban asphalt desert that is the nation's capital.

The center of Washington is reminiscent of that biblical capital city of Jerusalem. Within view is King Herod's palace at 1600 Pennsylvania Avenue; all about are the legions of Mary Magdalenes on sidewalks and church grounds; the church floors are crowded with the contemporary "leper colony" of homeless; the Pharisees at worship, led by Caiaphas the high priest. It is the scene on which the entire biblical cast of characters is present—from Amos to John the Baptist to Judas—and the salvation story of birth, life, death, and resurrection of Jesus is a daily occurrence.

The situation in any city is the scarcity of space—safe space!—for the literally "maddening crowd" who seek shelter and refuge from the violence of systemic powers and anarchic predators of the streets. For Luther Place, that need reached a crisis point with the process of "deinstitutionalization" that has resulted in tens of thousands of mentally ill persons being released from hospitals without adequate support systems in place. In the midst of a freezing winter the decision was made, not whether or not we should open the doors of Luther Place, but whether we would be faithful to God's mandate to "welcome the stranger," the sojourner in our midst, even as we too have been rescued by Yahweh, who is our refuge and strength, our "mighty fortress."

The ministry of hospitality deserves some biblical exposition, however scanty, because it is the key to Luther Place's identity as a theological expression on its 36,000 square feet in the heart of Washington, D.C. Hospitality is too frequently defined as meaning only social entertaining. When viewed in the context of history, however, the word gives much insight into our relationships with our fellow human beings.

As a concept, hospitality is acceptable and palatable to Luther Place. It is as American as apple pie. Yet it has radical implications that are inexhaustible and ultimate.

To be hospitable is to convert the *hostis* into a *hospes* (the enemy into a guest). It is to create free and fearless space where brotherhood and sisterhood can be formed and fully experienced. Hospitality is a relationship between host and guest that provides enough freedom for both to reveal their most precious gifts and to bring new life to each other. Luther Place strives to be a hospice, a nonthreatening, nonhostile environment where people are called to change, but at the same time are accepted as they are. This need will always be with us, for hospitality stems from the basic need of all people to be and to feel at home.

The idea of giving as a host and yet receiving more in return is a repeated theme of hospitality appearing throughout history. Always it is a dynamic process involving such a dynamic shifting of roles that it is difficult to discern who is hosting whom. Luther Place, beginning with an examination of the concept of hospitality in connection with the creation of the world and early Jewish and Greek history, moved on to look at how hospitality was a concept demonstrated in the lifestyle of Jesus and the early church. After examining hospitality as a celebrated theme throughout history, Luther Place Memorial Church then responded to the need for hospitality within the hostile environment of a major central intersection at the capital's crossroads.

Planet Earth—Our First Hospice/Refuge

The concept of hospitality first emerged along with the creation story written down by the Hebrew people. We must remember that this was written in retrospect by the people of Israel in an effort to explain their own beginnings. The creation story presents the idea that the earth and all the living creatures within it were viewed as a gift given by Yahweh to man and woman. Jewish tradition declares not only that the environment is a gift, but also that human existence is a gift. According to this perspective, the world was created by God as a hospice for man and woman. God was the host, and they were the guests. Their position as guests was not only one of being blessed by the gifts of the Creator, but along with the blessing, they were given responsibility.

This responsibility came from the biblical concept that they were created in God's image. They were put here to represent God's own sovereign authority on earth. They were to maintain creation as a faithful steward would. They were to represent God's sovereign power, but always under God's sovereignty. They were not to "own" as much as they were to be stewards, trustees, of those creations given to them by the supreme host, Yahweh, who was the giver of all life.

The mandate given to man and woman to "have dominion over the fish of the sea, and over the birds of the air and over every living thing that moves upon the earth" (Gen. 1:28) probably means that they were to care for all living creation with responsible, hospitable attitudes. They were to act as trustees of the creation around them, just as the creation was to be a hospice for them—a hospice given by the all-providing host.

The theme of the earth as hospice and of us, its creatures, as guests of God and hosts to one another is reiterated in the "jubilee" law of the Hebrews. This law proclaimed that every 50 years people were to return to their original family property, debts were to be remitted, slaves were to be set free, and the soil was to be left fallow (Lev. 25:8-17,20-21,29-31). This law shows that the idea of land being something that is "on lease" rather than something owned was not a new one. Land and the resources that come from it were not to be monopolized by a few but were to be shared by many.

Hospitality in Ancient Civilizations

Hospitality as reflected in the Hebrew creation story is seen also in the life of other ancient Semites, as well as among the ancient Greeks. Hospitality to the Greeks always held an aura of mystery, an aura that came from the suspicion that one of the strangers or guests visiting may be a god and that the host would be rewarded or punished according to his or her treatment of the visitor.

Traveling was rare in those days, except by people on a religious pilgrimage or by criminals escaping the law. Temples offered criminals security and pilgrims freedom to come and go as they wished. Some archeologists and historians think that temples were the first inns to be developed. If this was the case, then very early in history religion and hospice became interconnected.

The Greek language itself brings to the surface an interesting aspect of hospitality and shows the depth of knowledge that Greeks had concerning human dynamics. The Greek word for *host* and *guest* is the same word, *xenos,* showing that oftentimes a role reversal took place between host and guest. It was difficult to discern which was which. Another Greek word, the one for hospitality (*philoxenia,* "love of strangers"), implies that one is always ready to serve and care for those who are strangers and pass his or her way. The Latin word for hospitality also holds an interesting implication. The word *hospes,* which means both "stranger" and "enemy," brings in the aspect of risk involved in being hospitable. When people are truly hospitable, they are willing to accept hosting a total stranger, not knowing whether that person is friend or enemy.

The showing of hospitality was also highly valued in the Bedouin culture, especially since their home was in the desert. An oasis, or stopping place, was a mutual gift all desert people could offer each other. Among the Bedouin even one's enemy was to be protected and treated hospitably while he was within a host's tent.

There were many rules that grew up around hospitality, and one of these was that the host was to identify himself and keep the conversation running smoothly without asking that the guest identify himself or speak. Only after the guest's needs, such as food and rest, were filled was he expected to respond with a story; but even then he did not have to say if he was friend or foe. Abraham, in Genesis 18, is a prime example of such a host. He is visited by two mysterious strangers; and without knowing who they are, he extends a warm welcome, offering himself as their servant and preparing for them a magnificent feast. They then tell him who they are and proceed to confirm God's promise that he is to be the father of a great nation and that his wife, Sarah, is to be with child. Here, as so frequently in the host-guest relationship, the roles are reversed: Abraham becomes the guest, and his guests become the hosts as the gifts of salvation are exchanged.

The Israelite tradition is full of such stories. Elisha was shown hospitality by the Shunammite woman who had a small room built for his use whenever he was passing through that area of the country. She, his hostess, was blessed with a son through the prayers of Elisha. He, her guest, became her host through his act of concern. Each was guest of the other (2 Kings 4:8-37). Job serves as another example of an Old

Testament host. In defending himself before God, Job uses the fact that he has never turned away a stranger. He has always held an open house to the traveler (Job 31:32). This action again points to the high value the Semites placed on hospitality.

Along with the theme of hospitality in Jewish history, there is also the related idea that the powerless are to be given justice. The powerless, in fact, are all those oppressed by society—they are the poor and all those unable to provide for themselves through normal means. They are those who have temporarily had their rightful place taken from them in the hospice made for them by God. Isaiah says:

> Cease to do evil,
> learn to do good,
> seek justice,
> correct oppression;
> defend the fatherless,
> plead for the widow.
>
> (Isa. 1:15-17)

Pursuing justice can mean to identify so deeply with the oppressed and powerless of society that it is difficult to discern who is doing the hosting and who is being a guest. Host and guest are one because of the gifts they offer each other. Scripture says nothing of what sociologists today call upward mobility. Instead, it calls for the reverse—a downward pilgrimage.

Hospitality, too, was implicitly commanded by the Lord when he gave the law that the harvesters were not to be so efficient in their job that they did not leave some of the crop for the poor, the earth-guests in need (Deut. 24:19; Lev. 19:9-10, 23:22; Ruth 2:1-3). Hospitality is best exemplified in the life and witness of Jesus Christ, who, being God's incarnated flesh, was both the supreme host *and* guest of all who came in contact with him.

Jesus' View of Hospitality

Jesus from his very beginnings found "no room in the inn." This was simply a foreshadowing of the pattern of his life to come. He was a propertyless prophet with no place to lay his head, a wanderer who in his homelessness identified himself with the poor, the oppressed, the downcast, the sick, the exiled, and the poorly received of society.

Jesus, host and guest to people from all social classes, had a clear perception of what his hosts or guests needed, and he gave according to their needs. This perception was part of Jesus because he had a clear picture of who he was and felt at home with himself. He had no concealed agendas of his own; instead, he was free both to receive and confront those around him. He received others and allowed them the space to be who they were; but he also confronted them with his unambiguous presence, not hiding himself behind neutrality, but clearly and distinctly showing his ideas, his truth, and his life-style.

Jesus had true poverty of spirit, which made him an especially good host. He had no defenses and, therefore, could perceive no one as an enemy. He had nothing to defend. Jesus was not clinging anxiously to private property, knowledge, good name, or money. He was that one who had emptied himself. Much of Jesus' ministry took place through table fellowship. In fact, Jesus' first recorded miracle took place amidst feasting and fellowship. Table fellowship and hospitality shown to guests were of great importance among the Jewish people during the time of Christ.

The rules about table fellowship became a religious matter for the Pharisees, who had clearly defined ritualistic purifying acts. These included purifying oneself before eating, eating of pure food, and offering the proper tithes and blessings before partaking of food. Jesus, however, did not always conform to these rules. He was more interested in pushing beyond social, political, and religious boundaries and identifying with those people who recognized their needs and were willing not only to be hosts but also guests, though at the same time he did not ignore those who valued the table rules. Norman Perrin contended that it was Jesus' iconoclastic eating habits and comparisons that led to the crucifixion.[2] Luke 7:36-50 is an example of this; Jesus confronts Simon for being more concerned with ritual than with expressing true hospitality, as the "immoral" woman had done.

Jesus also sought fellowship with the outcasts of society, such as Zacchaeus the tax collector. Unobtrusively seeking out Jesus as host, Zacchaeus had the tables switched on him; Jesus sought fellowship at his table. Zacchaeus became a host, but, in so doing, found himself a guest of Jesus, who called Zacchaeus to be more than Zacchaeus had ever thought he could be. Zacchaeus responded to Jesus' hosting by returning stolen money fourfold to those from whom he had taken unfairly. Jesus' parables, stories, and teachings repeatedly emphasized the theme of hospitality. Along with this theme, however, is the emphasis on demonstrating justice to the poor. Jesus not only spoke out for justice but called the wealthy to repentance, denouncing wealth as an obstacle to one's being a sensitive host or a receptive guest.

The Meal as Hospitality

Regarding guest lists, Jesus instructed, "When you give a dinner or a banquet, do not invite your friends or your brothers or your kinsmen or rich neighbors, lest they also invite you in return, and you be repaid. But when you give a feast, invite the poor, the maimed, the lame, the blind, and you will be blessed, because they cannot repay you. You will be repaid at the resurrection of the just" (Luke 14;12-14).

Hosting is a selfless act done out of poverty of spirit without thought of reward. Hospitality is not entertaining. It is not a performance where one looks carefully to see how acts are applauded and received by guests. In the Gospel of Matthew, Jesus insists that to host the hungry, the thirsty, the stranger, the prisoner, the sick, and the naked is to host Christ himself (Matt. 25:31-46). To respond as a host in this way will bring salvation to the giver.

Though Jesus was guest many times throughout his lifetime, his supremacy as host is brought out in his invitation: "Come to me all who labor and are heavy laden, . . . and I will give you rest. Take my yoke [a yoke of forsaking all] upon you. . . and you will find rest for your souls" (Matt. 11:28-30). You will find rest and refreshment for your psyche, body, and spirit. It is through being a guest of Christ that one receives the wholeness that enables one to give wholeness to other guests within this hospice world. Christ, in offering the gifts of the perfect host, does not push himself upon others. It is only when we invite him as a guest that he can and will give the perfect gift of the host that he is.

Jesus left with his followers many living examples of what hospitality can and should be. It is significant that at the close of his physical life he chose the fellowship table as the form of communion spent with his disciples. It was a way of telling his disciples again that being guests and hosts to one another is what his ministry was and is all about. Along with the symbols of bread and wine as the brokenness of his body, there is also a call to the celebration of life. It is a celebration that can grow only out of the realization that one must accept the death and responsibility of being a guest of God—dying to the smallness of ourselves and living for responsibility by acting as hosts to those around us, stranger or foe.

Celebration also comes in the receiving of the gift of the host of Jesus at the Eucharist. As we give ourselves in death, he gives us the gift of life—a gift given in abundance so that we too may give to others. The Lord's Supper is so much an experience of receiving and giving that the mutuality of giver and receiver, host and guest, realizes itself in oneness. Table fellowship is not just a personal act between God and the individual person; instead, it is a corporate act of fellowship where hospitality is complete.

Hence, in worship at Luther Place, the centrality of the meal, the Eucharist, is thanksgiving. It is the source from which all our hospitality flows. It is where Christ, the host of hosts, meets his people. Jesus' imaginative use of the meal foreshadowed an event all Judaism looked forward to, namely, the marriage feast of the Lamb—the initiation of the final kingdom—the eternal messianic banquet. Here again the concept of host-guest relationships was part of scriptural imagery.

The early church and the teaching of the Epistles emphatically emphasize hospitality as a major theme. The early church, according to Acts, "devoted themselves to the apostles' teaching and fellowship, to the breaking of bread and the prayers. And fear came upon every soul; and many wonders and signs were done through the apostles. And all who believed were together and had all things in common; and they sold their possessions and goods and distributed them to all, as any had need. And day by day, attending the temple together and breaking bread in their homes, they partook of food with glad and generous hearts, praising God and having favor with all the people" (Acts 2:42-47a).

The sharing of God's gifts with those in need to the point of selling all one's possessions was not an unusual response to the call of Christ. Again, identification with the poor of the earth was part of the hospitality conceptualized by early Christians, and it remains a challenge for today's churches (2 Cor. 8:13-14; James 2:14-17; 1 John 3:16-17).

Hospitality through an Interreligious Base

Hospitality is done through an interreligious base and Lutheran Volunteer Corps gleaned from campuses to staff ministries. Most of Luther Place and its N Street Village ministries operate from an interreligious base that produces synergistic results, not unlike Jesus' multiplication of loaves and fishes, that would not be possible if these ministries were attempted unilaterally as the acts of a single Lutheran congregation.

Our church building and its contiguous block of townhouses shelter the full spread of human beings described in Matthew 25: "I was hungry and you gave me food, I was thirsty and you gave me drink, I was a stranger and you welcomed me, I was naked and you clothed me, I was sick and you visited me, I was in prison and you came to me" (vv. 35-36). In this "urban kibbutz," even as we do unto the least of these, we do unto him. Such actions ironically result in our own enrichment, our salvation! Always, as we host, the tables are turned and we are blessed.

Again, whether it be through sponsoring Bread for the City (emergency food, clothing, and counseling center) or whether it be through directly opening our doors to the hundreds of homeless exiles seeking a haven with offering shelter, food, and warmth each night, it is only through a collage of diversified volunteers that care can be offered, that needs can be met and that life can be affirmed on such low budgets. Each action becomes living reenactments of the miracles of multiplying the loaves and fishes, of changing water into wine, and of giving life to the "dead."

Each of the following ministries has one or more full-time coordinators, "adequate" facilities, and numbers of interfaith volunteers to provide food, clothing, medical supplies and prescriptions: Bread for the City and Zacchaeus Medical Clinic, reinforced by resident hospices such as Sarah House, Bethany House, Dietrich Bonhoeffer House, Deborah's Place, Raoul Wallenberg House, and others in the making.

Refuge as Evangelism

Each of these previously mentioned acts of hospitality is our evangelism. That is, each act is a "sanctification of God's name" by aiding us to become more and more one with the "least of these" and by providing us the way for doing the work of justice in coalition with any and all others of like mind or motivation.

The Hebrew concept for such actions is Kiddush ha-Shem—"To sanctify God's name by bearing witness in body, mind, soul and spirit to the difference that faith makes. These actions are done amidst the idolatries of the world even unto martyrdom."[3] By evangelism we mean to exemplify (not impose) the presence of God; and as such, it is our intention to be a light amidst the darkness of our nation's capital, a light such as Isaiah metaphorically envisioned and one such as Jesus incarnationally lived out. Thomas Circle, Washington, D.C., and the world desperately need such evangelistic illumination to give light in the midst of darkness.

We are called and baptized into a covenantal communion in Christ—receiving the Bread of Life around our altar tables, to be broken and shared with the people of God in the communion circle encompassing our city and the world in which we live. The ongoing reenactment and living out of sacramental Thanksgiving, being hosted and serving as surrogate hosts of the Host of hosts—that is for us the Christ-life. That is our strategy at Thomas Circle amidst incest, violence, and prostitution of every sort; amidst hunger and homelessness, wretchedness and decay.

If the example of Jesus means anything to us Christians, then our instincts must be pastoral, not exploitative nor self-serving. Within the open space that is created by a congregation's hospitable life-style, movement can take place, a flow that ultimately results in the embrace of the Shepherd and his homeless sheep, of the lost and the found. In reality, this embrace includes us all, and results in new lives that are healed and restored to harmony and wholeness with their creative source, Yahweh, in whose creation we are all guests, pilgrims, and sojourners.

Again, this experience in a center-city metropolitan ministry is not complete, nor is our future assured. We are in God's providence and living in the afterglow of Easter. It is that truth that enables us to face our own death as a congregation, should faithfulness require that, even as we live every day in the midst of Washington's dead and dying. Yet it is the victory over death that is celebrated around the altar table in the presence of Christ, and it is that triumphant event that enables, lifts, and inspires a congregation that by every criteria should have expired long ago. The Eucharist is central: it is the Source.

Consequently, Luther Place cannot, dare not, and will not die when it is so critically needed by the homeless of Washington, D.C., at Thomas Circle. Where would God's people go? What would they call "home" in this neighborhood? The White House with its ultra-security insulation? The elitist American Medical Association or the National Rifle Association? The Soviet Embassy with its shuttered windows and tomblike atmosphere? *The Washington Post?* The Justice Department? Housing and Urban Development? The Federal Bureau of Investigation? Holiday Inns? Garfinckel's Department Store? Where?

The truth is that there is no place to call home except that place where the Host offers eternal hospitality to the homeless flock. Luther Place must be that place. Simply a hospice. It is to be a shelter, an oasis, a refuge from the harsh environment of our capital's asphalt desert, a place where our own itinerant Savior can be at home and welcome outcasts, embracing exiles, those urban nomads who wander through life "restless until they find their rest in Him" (Augustine, *Confessions* 1), at his banquet with their ever-present Host.

14

BIBLE AND MISSION IN THE SUBURBAN CONGREGATION

Larry A. Hoffsis

On the evening of that day, the first day of the week, the doors being shut where the disciples were, for fear of the Jews, Jesus came and stood among them and said to them, "Peace be with you." When he had said this, he showed them his hands and his side. Then the disciples were glad when they saw the Lord. Jesus said to them again, "Peace be with you. As the Father has sent me, even so I send you." And when he had said this, he breathed on them, and said to them, "Receive the Holy Spirit. If you forgive the sins of any, they are forgiven; if you retain the sins of any, they are retained."

Now Thomas, one of the twelve, called the Twin, was not with them when Jesus came. So the other disciples told him, "We have seen the Lord." But he said to them, "Unless I see in his hands the print of the nails, and place my finger in the mark of the nails, and place my hand in his side, I will not believe."

Eight days later, his disciples were again in the house, and Thomas was with them. The doors were shut, but Jesus came and stood among them, and said, "Peace be with you." Then he said to Thomas, "Put your finger here, and see my hands; and put out your hand, and place it in my side; do not be faithless, but believing." Thomas answered him, "My Lord and my God!" Jesus said to him, "Have you believed because you have seen me? Blessed are those who have not seen and yet believe."

Now Jesus did many other signs in the presence of the disciples, which are not written in this book; but these are written that you may believe that Jesus is the Christ, the Son of God, and that believing you may have life in his name.

(John 20:19-31)

1. *The Jury Is Still Out on the Suburban Congregation*

It seemed as though a decision had already been rendered regarding the suburban church when Gibson Winter wrote *The Suburban Captivity of the Churches.* His decision anticipated that the churches in the suburbs would continue to forsake their true mission, which is to follow their Lord in serving the world, and instead would remain self-serving country clubs. Winter called them "introverted churches." "The introverted church is one which puts its own survival before its mission, its own identity above its task, its internal concerns before its apostolate, its rituals before its ministry."[1] According to Winter, it was in the second great American migration (the first being from the rural areas to the urban), the movement from the urban to the suburban, that the suburban churches had become exclusive and privatistic and had developed "social amnesia"—they had conveniently forgotten the people and problems of the city and had no intention of having their memory revived. "Beyond their own survival, the churches evince little sense of their task in the metropolis . . . ."[2] Scott Donaldson, in *The Suburban Myth,* and many other writers joined the critique and supported what seemed to be an obvious verdict. But Winter wrote in 1962, and the jury was still out.

Glowingly, Winter had begun his third chapter, "The Churches as Fellowship and Missions," with this sentence: "The mark of the primitive church was social inclusiveness—rich and poor, Jew and gentile, slave and free."[3] But Winter neglected to mention that the primitive church which Jesus visited behind locked doors on two occasions—the day of his resurrection and one week later—was also a church held in captivity by its own fears, and, furthermore, was hardly at that point the model of inclusiveness and mission-mindedness. On that church, too, the jury was still out.

Already by 1968, in his book *Protestantism in Suburban Life,* Frederick Shippey was seeing signs of a different outcome. At least he was sympathetic with the congregations in the suburbs. "For the genuinely

Christian person suburbia constitutes a real test of faith. Material advantages and attractive secular dimensions make it not an easy place in which to live as a Christian."[4] In the concluding paragraph of his book, he included this sentence: "The church has proved a redemptive force in suburbia over and over again." Nonetheless, the jury was still out.

In preparation for this chapter, I decided to conduct my own unscientific information-gathering from some suburban congregations regarding their understanding and practice of mission. In a letter to each of the 19 bishops of the American Lutheran Church, I requested from each district the names and addresses of 5-10 suburban congregations in which there might be an interplay of "Bible" and "mission." To these suburban congregations I sent an information-gathering instrument which ended with five questions. The first of those concluding questions read: "What, if anything, is unique about mission practice in the suburban context?"

Pastors of these suburban congregations quite honestly acknowledged all and more of the conditions Winter had identified, conditions which hinder the church's understanding and carrying out its mission as servant of Christ.

People living in the suburbs are an extremely mobile group. For the suburbanite, mobility means rootlessness and restlessness, a lack of extended family nearby and a longing for fellowship. For the suburban community, mobility creates a certain instability. For the suburban congregation, mobility requires motivating the church members to participate in projects of mission for which they may only do the planting and likely will not see the fruition.

Suburbanites are achievement-oriented. They live under the pressure to produce and with the fear of not "making it." The fact that they do live in the suburbs is one evidence that they have "made it," and yet, the frustration level can be very high. One of the pastors wrote: "For people in the suburbs, it is not a question of survival but a question of meaning." Another commented: "As one inner-city pastor told me years ago in Atlanta: 'The people I work with live with the illusion that if they can move to suburbia, life will have meaning. You work with people who have gotten there and still find themselves wanting and searching.' "

The people in suburbia are active people who can afford, and want to provide, every educational, athletic, and social opportunity to their families. They are very busy and are not immune from the "me-ism" of the day. "What's in it for me?" and "Do I have time?" are often questions that take priority over the fundamental question, "What is the mission of the church?"

A natural exclusivity and conservatism rises to protect the suburbanites' identity and possessions. On their own, they may not be aware that their homogeneity and isolation from the city is robbing them of a different kind of riches—variety in color, culture, and life-style.

Yet, for all these potential hindrances to mission, there was abundant evidence in the responses to the questionnaire that contemporary suburban congregations not only achieve a vision of their biblically mandated mission, but, like the apostles, do unlock the doors and embark upon that mission.

2. Suburban Congregations Need Love, Too

It should be obvious that before there can be a mission to the world *through* the suburban congregation, there must first be a mission *to* the suburban congregation itself.

Jesus brought no critique to the infant New Testament church, a church which had been so highly privileged in its training, so laden with expectation for its vision, and yet had failed so miserably. Jesus doesn't seem to register the disappointment we would expect over their "suburban captivity." He must know that before they can bring love to others, they themselves need to experience the love which will bring forgiveness and reinstatement, melt away their fears, and bring them peace. Such love he shows by pointing them to its evidence—the scars he bears in his body. Such love brings back into fellowship all those who, at the time of the crucifixion, had scattered in the face of the difficult task—including Thomas.

Perhaps Jesus even now is less concerned with the critique of the suburban church than with the love which he knows can bind suburban individualists into a fellowship. One pastor responded to my survey with these lines: "Fellowship is critical. The rapidity of change has left people wondering about their worth as persons. Self-esteem is at a low ebb. The gospel, which affirms our worth and value as children of God, is especially needed."

Quite evidently, according to the responses I received, suburban congregations have made fellowship a primary concern. And rightly so. To meet the challenges of mobility and resultant rootlessness, achievement-orientation and the question of meaning, busyness and necessity for prioritizing, suburban churches have established a multiplicity of small groups within the congregation.

These groups are not simply for socializing, as the term *fellowship* sometimes implies. They have nothing to do with images attached to the pejorative label "country club." These are care and support groups, some of them traditional, like the prayer chain and groups to prepare meals for a family at the time of death, but others bold new ventures designed to communicate the peace of Christ during frightening situations, as when a fellow member loses a job, experiences divorce, or learns that a child will be mentally or physically handicapped. Persons in such situations, who in the past were met by judgmental and further isolating action, are now drawn into a fellowship with the same restorative gestures of peace used by Jesus to bring together the isolated disciples. The congregations reported many other support groups, especially for that ever-growing number of suburbanites, the singles—both never-marrieds and widows. Using the biblical concept "family of God," and the sense of belonging stemming from that concept, congregations view such groups as part of their mission to the residents in suburbia.

Many congregations in suburbia, having heard the charge of exclusivism, and knowing that the adjective is too often accurate, have become quite intentional with the biblical injunction to "show hospitality" (Heb. 13:2). Another scripture passage, often reported in this connection is Gal. 6:2, "bear one another's burdens."

In stressing this mission to the congregation a lost dimension of priesthood of all believers is being recovered. Congregations which seriously practice hospitality and bear one another's burdens well know that these pastoral functions cannot be done by the clergy or leadership alone. The priesthood of all believers has been with us for a long time, but I had not noted its application to the function of hospitality and care until conducting this survey. Of course, such a mission by all members requires both trust and training of the laity, both of which seem to be in ample supply. Congregation after congregation noted the importance of such training programs for laity as the Stephen Series, training provided for lay-care teams by seminaries or training programs of a congregation's own devising.

It is a new and thrilling concept for members of suburban churches to find that the nuclear or biological family (often consisting of one) is not the final destination of congregational mission activity (as might be expected in the conservative suburbs) but that the new family, the church family, is thereby made solid enough to serve as the springboard for mission through the congregation to the community.

3. Suburban Congregations Have Much to Give

In the questions I asked of the suburban congregations, I gave no definition of "mission" but rather invited the responders to work with their own definition. To my request that each congregation list and give a narrative description of its mission activities, I was surprised by how little there was in the lists for the congregation's own benefit. Where such internal activities were listed, as in the various care and support groups, it was often for the purpose of building church fellowship, so that, from this group, ministry to others might be extended.

It was after Jesus had restored the fellowship of his disciples by means of his peace that he reissued the missionary directive which he, in various formulations, had given before. In the Easter evening meeting he put it this way: "As the Father sent me, even so I send you" (John 20:21). It was obvious from the lists of mission projects that the suburban congregations had also been listening to this missionary directive.

There seemed to be less of the introversion so obvious to Gibson Winter more than two decades ago. Indicators abounded that the congregations were attempting to face outward. For the self-indulged living in the suburbs of whom a pastor wrote, "we must provide the way for them to get out of self and in the lives of others," such ways were being provided.

When writing about their people, pastors of suburbanites noted that they are for the most part professional people, well-educated and well-paid, with more than the average of this world's goods. They are often the movers and shakers of the community, having influence as well as affluence. Suburban congregations have tremendous assets.

Many of the congregations felt that their role was first of all a matter of doing the best job possible to raise funds for projects to be administered by someone else, whether those be inner-city food and clothing pantries, contributions to Lutheran Social Service agencies, world hunger appeals, or missionary sponsorships. Every effort was made to avoid any paternalistic or superior attitudes in these missionary stewardship efforts.

But, above all, the suburban congregations view their greatest resource less in financial terms than in terms of their people. When such skilled persons glimpse the vision of Christ's mission, they become valuable assists to national and district commissions as well as shapers of the missionary effort in their own community.

The survey reported a keen interest in establishing relationships with the cities. In this interest, at least, lies the hope expressed by Gibson Winter that suburban churches would finally break out of their captivity and become churches for the metropolis.

"Part of the mission [of the suburban church] . . . is to continue to challenge the people to look beyond the property line, beyond themselves, beyond their mortgages, beyond their vocations to see the inclusive marketplace of the world. In a sense, our ministry is to those imprisoned by their own fears." So wrote a pastor whose list and narrative description of the congregation's missionary activities was designed to do more than *look* beyond. It was calculated to *send* beyond. In the linkage between the suburban and urban contexts of ministry one can behold "Visions of an Inclusive Church," to quote the title and note the substance of a 1984 document prepared by the American Lutheran Church's Office of Church in Society.

Congregations who clearly hear the Lord say, "So I send you," interpret that mandate to include linking with churches in urban areas, with ecumenical efforts, and even extending to establishing partner congregations in countries as far away as the Soviet Union. In such partnering, prayer weeks for peace in local congregations take on a quite different quality than the peace petitions in the general prayer.

4. Getting from Bible to Mission

I had asked each pastor in the survey to attempt to identify the vehicle that moved the mission directive from the Bible to its actual expression in the congregation's ministry.

On two points there was complete agreement. The first was that all true mission grows out of the Bible, that without the Bible there can be no mission, and that with the Bible there can be no escaping mission involvement. The second point was also unanimous: the most effective way to communicate the Bible mandates to the congregation for action is through adult education. Preaching was deemed also to be very important because through preaching greater numbers of people are reached. Nonetheless, adult education was even more important because of its opportunity for dialog and discovery.

This should not be surprising, for in a study prepared by Milo and Mark Brekke entitled "Results of Research concerning Evangelistic Gains and Inactive Losses of Members of the American Lutheran Church,"[5] this finding was presented: "Percentage of confirmed members enrolled in adult education classes in 1980 correlated significantly with congregational rate of evangelistic gain." The same could no doubt be said in a more general way regarding a congregation's understanding and involvement in mission.

The congregations in the survey reported that they therefore offer many opportunities for adult Bible study each week. Not only do they have multiple choices of courses on Sunday morning but they also provide weekday sessions. It is important that the classes be structured in such a way that the class members may become involved directly with the text through small group discussions. Many of the congregations reported that they used studies which proceed according to a plan of some duration, and which give an overview, like the Bethel Series or the Search Weekly Bible Study series.

A significant number of congregations also hold a planning retreat with their leaders for the purpose of drafting a congregational mission statement each year. The retreat begins with the Bible study, so that the congregational leaders may have opportunities to hear the Lord of the church speak as he did to the first Christians when he gave them the center of his missionary message, namely, the ministry of forgiveness and reconciliation. I was impressed with the mission statements that many of the pastors included. The obvious advantage of such written statements is that they make the congregation struggle with the questions "What does this word of God mean for us?" and "How shall we make that answer visible and intentional?"

5. *More Than Words, It Is "The Word"*

I was interested in what specific sections of Scripture were guiding our congregations into mission today. Following the listing of mission activities and their narrative description, I asked that the passage of Scripture which led them to this activity be cited. My summary page was full of scriptural citations. However, it will be of no surprise to anyone when I reveal that the two scripture references mentioned time and time again are the Great Commission, Matt. 28:19-20, and the parable of the sheep and the goats, Matt. 25:31-46. It is awesome to contemplate the power of these words from God for generating mission linkages of worldwide scope. But then we would expect such from these words: "Go therefore and make disciples of *all nations* . . ." (Matt. 28:19).

In completing this final question of the survey, however, many pastors felt obliged to note that there was often no direct correlation from a specific reading to a specific mission thrust. What then inspired it? It was contact with Jesus, the Word, who gave birth to the mission. So, a pastor wrote, "the church in suburbia must provide a place for the hearing of the one Word, the Word that shapes all our words."

That was the experience which brought the jury back to give its verdict on the primitive church. Before the visit with the risen Lord, the faithfulness to the Lord's mission remained in doubt. Locked doors, introversion, exclusiveness, the priority of security, captivity because of fear—all these seemed to have set a sad course for the early church. On their own the disciples would never have removed the locks. They would rather have improved them.

People in the suburbs with their own potential for captivity are also like that. As we view what some think of as the "good life," we know that we will not with the passing years become less conservative, but likely more so. It is impossible to break out in mission on our own. We need a visit from the Lord, an encounter with the living Word.

In the suburbs it is easy to develop a human view regarding how we got where we are. "We have paid our dues elsewhere, and now we deserve to be here!" So goes the reasoning. We can even view the resurrected Christ by the rewards system. He went to the cross. He paid his dues. Now he deserves the golden crown with its jewels. He deserves a place of privilege at the right hand of God from which place of safety he rightly directs the affairs of God's realm. Having defeated death, Christ is envisioned as a military hero, wearing a uniform, with medals displayed—the purple heart (Wasn't he wounded?) and the bronze star (Wasn't he brave?).

When Jesus comes into our churches, in the suburbs or elsewhere, he looks much as he did before, still serving, still identifying with those "out there" who need him. We reach out to touch the medals—the star, but he takes our hand and places it instead on the scar. It is not then studying words of the Bible but getting in touch with the *Word* of the Bible that moves the suburban church to leave its captivity, to unlock the doors and be sent into this world in the same way the Father sent Jesus.[6]

ABBREVIATIONS

FS	Festschrift
IDB	*Interpreter's Dictionary of the Bible* (New York and Nashville: Abingdon, 1962)
IRM	*International Review of Missions*
ITQ	*Irish Theological Quarterly*
LBW	*Lutheran Book of Worship*
NTS	*New Testament Studies*
RSV	Revised Standard Version
SBT	Studies in Biblical Theology
TDNT	*Theological Dictionary of the New Testament*, trans. G. Bromiley (Grand Rapids: Eerdmans, 1964–1976)
TEV	Today's English Version (Good News Bible)

NOTES

Introduction

1. Karl Barth, *The Word of God and the Word of Man,* trans. Douglas Horton (New York: Harper and Row, 1957), p. 119.
2. Karl Barth, *The Epistle to the Romans,* trans. Edwyn C. Hoskyns (New York: Oxford University Press, 1933), p. 37.
3. Ibid., pp. 37-38.
4. 2 Peter 3:13, TEV.

Chapter 1. Fretheim: Mission in the Old Testament

1. The following are suggested supplementary readings for themes discussed in this chapter:
   L. Croner and L. Klenicki, eds., *Issues in the Jewish-Christian Dialogue: Jewish Perspectives on Covenant, Mission and Witness* (New York: Paulist, 1979).
   R. Martin-Achard, *A Light to the Nations: A Study of the Old Testament Conception of Israel's Mission to the World* (Edinburgh: Oliver and Boyd, 1962).
   G. E. Mendenhall, "Mission," in *IDB* 3:404-406.
   M. H. Pope, "Proselyte," in *IDB* 3:921-931.
   H. H. Rowley, *The Missionary Message of the Old Testament* (London: Carey, 1944).
   D. Senior and C. Stuhlmueller, *The Biblical Foundations for Mission* (Maryknoll, N.Y.: Orbis, 1983).
   C. Westermann, *The Praise of God in the Psalms* (Richmond: John Knox, 1965).
2. George Mendenhall, "Mission," p. 405.

Chapter 3. Harrisville: Paul

1. Cited from Chaim Stern, ed., *Gates of Repentance* (New York: Central Conference of American Rabbis, 1978), p. 262.
2. A. Dupont-Sommer, *The Essene Writings from Qumran,* trans. G. Vermes (Oxford: Blackwell, 1961), p. 326 (1Q *27* 15-17).

Chapter 4. Hoops: The Fourth Gospel

1. The ambiguity is apparent in the English and the Greek. Note also the textual problem involving the word *believe* (Greek, *pisteuō*); cf., e.g., the 26th ed. of the Nestle/Aland text of the Greek New Testament.
2. The term is used in a positive sense here.
3. Raymond Brown, *The Gospel according to John, I-XII* (Garden City, N.Y.: Doubleday, 1966), p. LXXVIII.
4. Thus far, the term *mission* has been used in a quite traditional sense, i.e., "being concerned with preaching the gospel to those who do not believe in Christ." That will be the primary meaning of the term as it is used below (the context will, at times, reveal variant meanings). Because the evangelist rarely makes direct statements about mission to outsiders, the writer has chosen to use *witness* as having a more flexible definition (cf. the subtitle to this chapter). The basic meaning of *witness* is "to give evidence in favor of Jesus." For discussion about indirect mission statements see Ferdinand Hahn, *Mission in the New Testament,* SBT 47 (London: SCM, 1965), pp. 19-20, 152ff., etc.
5. See Hahn, *Mission,* pp. 16, 137, 140, etc.
6. The explorations have led to significant results. Among others, see Donald Senior and Carroll Stuehlmueller, *The Biblical Foundations for Mission* (Maryknoll, N.Y.: Orbis, 1983), and James McPolin, "Mission in the Fourth Gospel," *ITQ* 36 (1969): 113-122.
7. Stephen Neill reminds us that "to some extent one's interpretation of the theology of the gospel will be affected by one's view of its origin," in *Jesus through Many Eyes* (Philadelphia: Fortress, 1976), p. 141. When one understands the context for many of the discussions in John, then one can readily perceive that anti-Semitism has no place in witnessing today.
8. Because of the condensed nature of this article, the terms *evangelist, author,* and *John* will be used interchangeably; it is not possible to examine here the intricacies of the question of authorship.
9. For positive results of such critical awareness, see Karl Paul Donfried, *The Dynamic Word* (San Francisco: Harper and Row, 1981), and Allen Verhey, *The Great Reversal: Ethics and the New Testament* (Grand Rapids: Eerdmans, 1984).
10. Edwin C. Hoskyns and Noel Davey, *The Riddle of the New Testament* (London: Faber and Faber, 1931), pp. 148-149.
11. See the careful description in R. H. Fuller, *A Critical Introduction to the New Testament* (London: Gerald Duckworth, 1971, reprint), pp. 17f.
12. Pheme Perkins, *The Gospel according to John* (Chicago: Franciscan Herald, 1978), pp. 35-37.

13. See particularly his *Community of the Beloved Disciple* (New York: Paulist, 1979).
14. Raymond Brown, *John,* 1:XXXIVff.
15. Three Johannine texts, 9:22; 12:42; and 16:2, are particularly significant; see his *History and Theology in the Fourth Gospel,* rev. ed. (Nashville: Abingdon, 1979), especially chap. 2.
16. The modified Benediction is cited in ibid., p. 58.
17. Donfried, *Dynamic Word,* p. 17.
18. Martyn, *History and Theology,* especially chaps. 3 and 7.
19. Both are Series B texts for Lent, for the fourth and fifth Sundays, respectively; see *LBW,* p. 19.
20. Edwin Hoskyns, *The Fourth Gospel,* ed. F. N. Davey, 2nd ed. (London: Faber and Faber, 1947), p. 203.
21. See, e.g., Nils Dahl, *Jesus in the Memory of the Early Church* (Minneapolis: Augsburg, 1976), p. 102.
22. Many of John's writing techniques are apparent in this section, e.g., progress through misunderstandings, dialog into monolog, and double meanings. For one discussion, see Raymond Brown, *John,* 1:CXXXVf.
23. Many good popular expositions of this and other chapters have appeared recently. Among those to whom the writer is indebted is Robert E. Obach and Albert Kirk, *A Commentary on the Gospel of John* (New York: Paulist, 1981).
24. Ibid., p. 63.
25. From the Greek *hypsoō* ("lift up"), which has a double meaning for John: being lifted up on the cross, and being exalted.
26. Peter F. Ellis, *The Genius of John* (Collegeville, Minn.: Liturgical Press, 1984), particularly stresses this; see p. 56.
27. See the discussion below; the word *gave* in Greek here is *edoken* ("he really [or 'actually'] gave").
28. A concordance will show that the expression "God loved the *world*" is unusual in this Gospel. The reason seems to lie in the language and intent of the evangelist (see Brown, *John,* 1:133).
29. John uses other descriptions as well; cf. 12:32, "drawn" by Jesus. Cf. also Pheme Perkins, *John,* p. 36: "Although he wishes to affect the behavior of his readers, the Evangelist's metaphors cannot simply be interpreted as demands that we 'make a decision' for Christ. In fact, in a religious context, decision language is highly ambiguous.

    "We tend to associate circumstances with it that are under our control. Yet faith in the Fourth Gospel can hardly be associated with the exercise of will that is usually connoted by 'decide.' Use of such language about the Spirit in this chapter shows that, in some respect, the believer's faith is not his or her own creation. At the same time, those who do not heed the revelation are considered culpable."

30. For this interpretation of the word *Greeks* (RSV) see Brown, *John,* 1:466, and C. K. Barrett, *The Gospel according to John,* 2nd ed. (Philadelphia: Westminster, 1978), p. 421. This translation suggests a fulfillment of 12:19f. and sets the stage for 12:32; thus, the translation of the word is contextual.
31. Note the preceding passages, 2:4; 7:6; 8:20, where there are references to "my hour" not having come.
32. The love/hate language is simply first-century parlance about discipleship; it focuses on priorities. The Synoptics have similar language.
33. See Rudolf Bultmann, *Theology of the New Testament* (London: SCM, 1955), 2:48.
34. See also John 10:16; The evangelist uses the word *drawn,* rather than *called,* used in the Synoptics.
35. W. R. G. Loader, "The Central Structure of Johannine Christology," *NTS* 30 (1984): 189-191.
36. Peder Borgen, "God's Agent in the Fourth Gospel," in *Religions in Antiquity,* FS for E. R. Goodenough, ed. Jacob Neusner (London: E. J. Brill, 1968), pp. 137-148.
37. For a less elaborate study of specific aspects of this theme see K. H. Rengstorf, "*apostellō,*" in *TDNT,* 1:398-446.
38. McPolin, "Mission," pp. 113-122, especially p. 116.

Chapter 6. Huffman: Biblical Motifs in Modern Mission Theology

1. Emilio Castro, *Sent Free: Mission and Unity in the Perspective of Kingdom* (Geneva: World Council of Churches, 1985), p. 16.
2. Ibid.
3. Ibid.
4. Cf. Charles R. Taber, "Missiology and the Bible," *Missiology* 11 (1983): 241ff.
5. Cf. Samuel Excobar, "The Gospel and the Poor," in S. Escobar and John Driver, eds., *Christian Mission and Social Justice* (Scottdale, Pa.: Herald Press, 1978).
6. Taber, p. 242.
7. Ibid.
8. Ibid.
9. One measure of the change in the directional flow of theology is the rapidly increasing number of volumes of theology from Asia, Africa, and

Latin America that is being translated into English and German and made available to the Western theological world.

10. Cf. Gustavo Gutierrez, *A Theology of Liberation* (Maryknoll, N.Y.: Orbis, 1973), pp. 153ff.
11. Cf. Desmond Tutu, *Hope and Suffering* (Grand Rapids: Eerdmans, 1984), pp. 50ff.
12. A North American missionary seized in Guatemala not long ago was interrogated in great detail by the security forces concerning his interpretation of the story of the Exodus, since that was thought to be a key to his theological and political views. In Latin America the large and growing theological movement known as liberation theology represents such a perspective. The South African theologians who articulate an Exodus motif include Desmond Tutu, Allen Boesak, Manas Buthelezi, Zephaniah Kameetah, and T. Simon Farisani.
13. Cf. Gutierrez, p. 153.
14. Cf. ibid., pp. 153-160.
15. Cf. Tutu, pp. 48-61.
16. Orlando E. Costas, *The Integrity of Mission* (New York: Harper and Row, 1979), p. 62.
17. *Bangkok Assembly 1973: Minutes and Report of the Assembly of the CWME of the WCC, December 31, 1972 and January 9-12, 1973* (Geneva: World Council of Churches, 1973), p. 87. In his book on the assembly Arne Sovik gives voice to the difference of perspective and the breadth of meaning for the term *salvation* when he writes, "*Liberation* is the poor man's definition of salvation" (*Salvation Today* [Minneapolis: Augsburg, 1973]). Cf. Pauline Webb, *Salvation Today* (London: SCM, 1974). At least a part of this comprehensive view was foreshadowed in the *Mission Affirmations* adopted by the Lutheran Church–Missouri Synod in June, 1965, and available from Partners in Mission, P.O. Box 3786, St. Louis, MO 63122.
18. John R. W. Stott, *Christian Mission in the Modern World* (London: Falcon, 1975), p. 23.
19. Rodger C. Bassham, *Mission Theology* (Pasadena: William Carey Library, 1979), p. 233.
20. "A Declaration from the Synod," *IRM* 64.255 (1974): 313.
21. Cf. Robert McAfee Brown, *Unexpected News: Reading the Bible with Third World Eyes* (Philadelphia: Westminster, 1984), pp. 63ff.
22. Cf., for example, Frederick Herzog, *Justice Church* (Maryknoll: Orbis, 1980).

23. Waldron Scott, *Bring Forth Justice: A Contemporary Perspective on Mission* (Grand Rapids: Eerdmans, 1980), p. xv.
24. Ibid., p. xvi.
25. *Evangelism and Social Responsibility,* The Grand Rapids Report (Exeter: Pater Noster Press, 1982), p. 24.
26. *National Catholic Reporter,* May 17, 1985, p. 8.
27. Gutierrez, *Theology of Liberation,* p. 195.
28. Cf. John Eagleson and Philip Scharper, eds., *Puebla and Beyond* (Maryknoll: Orbis, 1979), p. 264. Cf. *The Church in the Present-Day Transformation of Latin America in the Light of the Council,* vol. 2, *Conclusions,* 2nd ed. (Washington, D.C.: Division for Latin America, U.S. Catholic Conference, 1968), pp. 191ff.
29. Emilio Castro, in an editorial in *IRM* 69 (October 1980—January 1981): 380.
30. Among the best are: Julio de Santa Ana, *Good News to the Poor* (Maryknoll: Orbis, 1979) and *Towards a Church of the Poor* (Maryknoll: Orbis, 1981); Ralph Doermann, *Biblical Concern for the Poor* (Minneapolis: Commission on Church and Society, The American Lutheran Church, 1972); Walter Pilgrim, *Good News to the Poor: Wealth and Poverty in Luke-Acts* (Minneapolis: Augsburg, 1981); and Richard D. N. Dickinson, *Poor, Yet Making Many Rich: The Poor as Agents of Creative Justice* (Geneva: World Council of Churches, 1983).
31. Among the most helpful are: Wolfgang Stegemann, *The Gospel and the Poor* (Philadelphia: Fortress, 1984) and L. Wm. Countryman, *The Rich Christian in the Church of the Early Empire* (New York and Toronto: Edwin Mellen, 1980); cf. also Norman Gottwald, ed., *The Bible and Liberation: Political and Social Hermeneutics* (a revised edition of *A Radical Religion Reader)* (Maryknoll: Orbis, 1983).
32. The Melbourne Conference of 1980 called the nonpoor churches "to become the churches in solidarity with the poor." In its recently published *Mission Principles and Priorities,* the Division for World Mission and Inter-Church Cooperation of The American Lutheran Church lists as its third major program priority "the development of holistic mission in the areas of deepest poverty and most oppressive injustice" (DWMIC, The ALC, 422 South Fifth Street, Minneapolis, MN 55415).
33. Cf. Mortimer Arias, "Evangelism and the Poor and the Oppressed," in *The Continuing Frontier: Evangelism* (New York: Lutheran Church in America, Division for World Mission and Ecumenism, 1984), p. 48.
34. John Dominic Crossan, *In Parables* (New York: Harper and Row, 1973), p. 23.

35. Costas, *Integrity of Mission,* p. 7.
36. Ibid.
37. "Section Reports: Melbourne Conference," *IRM* 69 (October 1980—January 1981): 408.
38. Ibid., p. 384.
39. Ibid., p. 401.
40. Ibid., p. 398.
41. Ibid., p. 400. Cf. Emilio Castro, *Sent Free*. This fine volume, based on Castro's doctrinal dissertation at Lausanne, gives a comprehensive treatment of the implications for mission of the motif of the kingdom.
42. "Section Reports: Melbourne Conference," *IRM* 69 (October 1980—January 1981): 397.
43. Johannes Verkuyl, *Contemporary Missiology: An Introduction,* trans. and ed. Dale Cooper (Grand Rapids: Eerdmans, 1978), p. 95.
44. Tim Huffman, "The Shape of Mission," *Trinity Seminary Review* 7:1 (Spring 1985): 9.
45. "Section Reports: Melbourne Conference," *IRM* 69:401.
46. Tutu, *Hope and Suffering,* p. 66.
47. "Section Reports: Melbourne Conference," *IRM* 69:401.
48. Lutheran World Federation, *Working Paper on Mission,* paragraph 49.
49. Ibid., paragraph 37.

Chapter 8. Larson: Bible and Mission in a Large Congregation.

1. Cf. Augsburg Confession, Article 7.
2. Quoted on the Augsburg Service Folder for Transfiguration Sunday, 1985.
3. *Worship as Pastoral Care* (Nashville: Abingdon, 1979), p. 97.
4. Augsburg Confession 5.
5. Martin Luther, "Eight Sermons by Dr. Martin Luther," trans. A. Steimle (Philadelphia: A. J. Holman, 1915), pp. 414-415.
6. Cf. Bonhoeffer: "But what does 'believing in the church' mean? We do not believe in an invisible church, nor in the kingdom of God existing in the church as *coetus electorum* [gathering of the elect]; but we believe that God has made the actual empirical church, in which the Word and the sacraments are administered, into his community, that it is the Body of Christ, that is, the presence of Christ in the world, and that according to the promise God's Spirit becomes effective in it. We believe in the church as the church of God and as the communion of saints, of those, that is, who are sanctified by God, but within the historical form of the empirical church. Thus we believe in the means of grace within the empirical church and hence in the holy congregation created by them. . . .

"We believe in the church not as an unattainable ideal, or one which has still to be attained, but as a present reality. What distinguishes Christian thinking from all idealist theories of community is that the Christian community is the church of God in every moment of history and it knows it will never attain perfection within the development of history. It will remain impure as long as history exists, and yet in this its actual form it is God's church" (Dietrich Bonhoeffer, *The Communion of Saints* [New York: Harper and Row, 1963], p. 197).

7. Commission for a New Lutheran Church, "Statement of Purpose" 1h. "A particular contribution of the Reformation was to stress the importance of daily life and work in the world" (CNLC Report of the Task Force on Theology, p. 8).
8. Augsburg Confession 16.
9. Ibid. 24.
10. *Baptism, Eucharist and Ministry,* Faith and Order Paper no. 111 (Geneva: World Council of Churches, 1982), p. 15.
11. Augsburg Confession 13.
12. *Baptism, Eucharist and Ministry,* p. 14.
13. Robert Worley, *Change in the Church: A Source of Hope* (Philadelphia: Westminster, 1971), pp. 59, 60.
14. Commission for a New Lutheran Church, "Statement of Purpose," 1k.
15. Eph. 2:10.
16. *Lutheran Book of Worship,* p. 153.

Chapter 9. Collinson-Streng and de la Tejera: Bible and Mission in a Hispanic Congregation

1. Symposium on Hispanic Ministries, Mexican-American Program, Perkins School of Theology, 1981.
2. See Orlando Costas, *The Integrity of Mission* (New York, Harper and Row, 1979), p. 12.
3. Virgilio P. Elizondo, *Christianity and Culture: An Introduction to Pastoral Theology and Ministry for the Bicultural Community* (Huntington, Ind., Our Sunday Visitor, 1975), p. 30.
4. See "Faith Expressions of Hispanics in the Southwest," Mexican-American Cultural Center, San Antonio, Texas, 1979, and Robert T. Trotter II and Juan Antonio Chavia, *Curanderismo: Mexican-American Folk Healing* (Athens: University of Georgia Press, 1981).
5. Frank Ponce, "Building Basic Christian Communities: Comunidades Eclesiales de Base in the U.S. Experience," in *Developing Basic Christian*

Communities: A Handbook (Chicago: National Federation of Priests' Councils, 1979).

Chapter 10. Thompson: Bible and Mission in the Rural Congregation

1. Peter Taylor Forsyth, *Positive Preaching and the Modern Mind* (Grand Rapids: Baker, 1980), p. 36.
2. Ibid., pp. 15, 108.
3. The *Book of Concord* (Philadelphia: Fortress, 1959), p. 31.
4. Smalcald Articles 3.12, in ibid., p. 315.
5. Ibid., p. 345.
6. Romans 5:6,8; 6:6,10-11.
7. Nils Dahl, *Jesus in the Memory of the Early Church* (Minneapolis: Augsburg, 1976).
8. Ibid., p. 15.
9. Quoted by F. Bente, *Historical Introduction to the Book of Concord* (St. Louis: Concordia, 1965).
10. George Bernanos, *Diary of a Country Priest* (Chicago: Thomas More, 1983), p. 19.
11. *Lutheran Book of Worship* (Minneapolis: Augsburg, and Philadelphia: Board of Publication, LCA, 1978,) p. 56.
12. Robert Jenson, *Story and Promise* (Philadelphia: Fortress, 1973), p. 193.
13. See Matt. 28:19-20; John 15:16-17; 16:12-15; 17:15-19; 20:21-23.
14. Paul Scherer, *The Word of God Sent* (Grand Rapids: Baker, 1977), pp. 17, 21.
15. Rom. 1:16-17.

Chapter 11. Pereya: A Biblical Perspective in a Multicultural Setting

1. *Trinity through the Years: 1890-1950 (Sixtieth Anniversary)* (privately published), p. 20.
2. Ibid., p. 29.
3. Lam. 2:25; 2 Kings 25:18-27. John Bright, *The Kingdom of God* (New York: Abingdon,1953), p. 129, notes that the population of Judah was more than 250,000 in the eighth century B.C. After the deportation in 597 B.C., the population was only 20,000.
4. John Bright, p. 130.
5. Ibid.
6. John H. Elliott and Ray Martin, *James, 1 and 2 Peter, Jude* (Minneapolis: Augsburg, 1982), pp. 60-61.
7. Joseph P. Fitzpatrick, *Puerto Rican American* (Englewood Cliffs, N.J.: Prentice-Hall), p. 2.

8. Marina Herrera, *Adult Education for the Hispanic Community.* (Washington, D.C.: National Conference of Diocesan Directors, 1984), p. 60.
9. James Cone, *For My People* (Maryknoll, N.Y.: Orbis, 1984).
10. Virgilio Elizondo is executive director of the Mexican-American Cultural Center (MACC), San Antonio, Texas.
11. It is interesting to read the entire excerpt quoted by Antonio S. Arroyo in *Prophets Denied Honor* (Maryknoll, N.Y.: Orbis, 1980), pp. 214-218; see also "Toward a National Hispano Church" by Padres Alberto Carrilo in the same book, pp. 154ff.
12. James Cone, *For My People,* pp. 166, 172-173.
13. The people come to the altar and humbly pray for an apartment, for healing, for their relatives, for jobs, for someone involved in alcoholism or drugs. Their prayers are very existential.
14. Severino Croatto, *Vox Evangelii* (Buenos Aires: Instituto Superior de Estudios Teológicos, 1984), p. 18.
15. Ibid., p. 11.
16. Segundo Galilea, *La teología de la liberacíon despúes de Puebla* (Bogota, Colombia: Coleccíon Iglesia Nueva, Indo-American Press Service, 1979), p. 17.

Chapter 13. Steinbruck: Bible and Mission in a Center-City Congregation

1. Walter Brueggemann, *Living toward a Vision* (Philadelphia: United Church Press, 1959), p. 15.
2. *Rediscovering the Teaching of Jesus* (New York: Harper and Row, 1967), pp. 102-106.
3. Seymour Siegel, "Jewish Self-Understanding," unpublished paper prepared for a consultation of Jewish-Lutheran understanding, Madison, Wisc., November 28, 1976.

Chapter 14. Hoffsis: Bible and Mission in the Suburban Congregation

1. Gibson Winter, *The Suburban Captivity of the Churches: An Analysis of Protestant Responsibility in the Expanding Metropolis* (New York: Macmillan, 1962), p. 2.
2. Ibid.
3. Ibid., p. 103.
4. Frederick A. Shippey, *Protestantism in Suburban Life* (Nashville: Abingdon, 1964), p. 3.

5. Draft prepared for the Division for Life and Mission in the Congregation, The American Lutheran Church (Minneapolis, 1982).
6. For further study see Winter, *The Suburban Captivity,* Shippey, *Protestantism,* and the following:

   Wilfred M. Bailey and William K. McElvaney, *Christ's Suburban Body* (Nashville: Abingdon, 1970).

   Scott Donaldson, *The Suburban Myth* (New York: Columbia University Press, 1969).

   Andrew M. Greeley, *The Church in the Suburbs* (New York: Sheed and Ward, 1959).

   William A. Holmes, *Tomorrow's Church: A Cosmopolitan Community* (Nashville: Abingdon, 1968).

   Donald L. Metz, *New Congregations: Security and Mission in Conflict* (Philadelphia: Westminster, 1967).

   Gaylord B. Noyce, *The Responsible Suburban Church* (Philadelphia: Westminster, 1970).

   W. Widick Schroeder, Victor Obernhaus, Larry A. Jones, and Thomas Sweetser, *Suburban Religion: Churches and Synagogues in the American Experience* (Chicago: Center for the Scientific Study of Religion, 1974).